PRAISE FOR
WORLD INVISIBLE

"Elegant, perceptive, and profound, *World Invisible* invites us into a timely and timeless reflection on the nature and mystery of the angels. In doing so, it teaches us not only to reflect in faith on the angelic world revealed in scripture, but also to take better stock of our own nature as spiritual animals made in the image of God, and of the invisible source of all created reality, human and angelic, who is God himself. The study of angels, as Fr. Saward notes, is ultimately an invitation to each of us to consider the contemplative vocation of the Christian, and our calling to eternal life with God. A wonderful book."

— **THOMAS JOSEPH WHITE**, OP, Rector, Angelicum, Rome

"*World Invisible: The Catholic Doctrine of the Angels* provides a synthesis of the perennial faith of Holy Church regarding God's incorporeal creatures. The reader is led along the way by the theology of St. Thomas Aquinas, Dante's poetry, and paintings by Sandro Botticelli, along with 20th-century Thomistic theologians such as Fr. Réginald Garrigou-Lagrange and Abbot Anscar Vonier. The book is thoughtfully crafted to benefit a wide readership. We learn about the creation of the angels and their subsequent acceptance or refusal of God's love. The angelic nature is described with clarity, including its intuitive mode of intellection that excludes mistakes and repentance. The holy angels find fulfillment in the praise and service of God, as illustrated by the traditional liturgy of Holy Church. The reader is assured that fallen angels and demons cannot harm us beyond what God's providence may allow, whereas holy angels actively foster our salvation. Finally, we are reminded that the Queen of the angels is our heavenly Mother, the Blessed Virgin Mary, true Mother of God. This enlightening book will help many become more familiar with the angels, for safer protection against demons and for more fruitful collaboration with our God-appointed heavenly guardians."

— **FR. ARMAND DE MALLERAY**, FSSP, author of *Vermeer's Angel*

"Fr. Saward has written a luminous, comprehensive, and truly beautiful guide to the angels — a challenging, rewarding, and spiritually important topic, yet one that is sadly neglected today. Making deft use of the witness of Scripture and Tradition, the Church Fathers, the Angelic Doctor, St. Thomas Aquinas, and the moving words of poets (especially Dante), the author acts as a reliable guide to what we can know, by reason and by faith, about the 'world invisible' — a world populated by myriad spirits in their varied ranks and tasks, divided into the holy angels and the demons, all of whom serve the purposes of Divine Providence and submit to Christ their King and the Virgin Mary their Queen. The best short book on the subject that has yet been written."

— **PETER A. KWASNIEWSKI**, author of *The Ecstasy of Love in the Thought of Thomas Aquinas*

"Astronomy discloses cosmic immensities and stunning beauties among the constellations, with trillions of galaxies and quadrillions of stars. But divine revelation discloses *angelic* constellations, incomparably more expansive in their majesty, and mysterious in their metaphysics. There is so much to ponder here that we should be grateful when yet another book on the angels appears — especially one as theologically fine-tuned and culturally cross-referenced as Fr. Saward's. He has positioned a fitting angelic canopy over his impressive array of publications."

— **SCOTT RANDALL PAINE**, author of *The Other World We Live In: A Catholic Vision of Angelic Reality*

WORLD · INVISIBLE

WORLD INVISIBLE

THE · CATHOLIC DOCTRINE · OF THE · ANGELS

JOHN SAWARD

Angelico Press

First published in the USA
by Angelico Press 2023
Copyright © John Saward 2023

For information, address:
Angelico Press, Ltd.
169 Monitor St.
Brooklyn, NY 11222
www.angelicopress.com

ppr 978-1-62138-950-7
cloth 978-1-62138-951-4

Book and cover design
by Michael Schrauzer

Ad honorem Beatae Mariae Deiparae
semper virginis
Reginae angelorum

For my family

CONTENTS

ACKNOWLEDGEMENTS

THIS BOOK HAS BEEN A LONG TIME IN the making. It started off in 2006 as talks given to the nuns of St Cecilia's Abbey at Ryde on the Isle of Wight. I am grateful to Mother Abbess for her invitation, and for the community's hospitality extended to me on that occasion and on other visits over many years. The talks were slowly transformed into the chapters of a book during times of study made possible only by the practical assistance of brother priests, the generosity and efficiency of the "home team" in the parish, and the loving support of my family. May Blessed Mary Ever-Virgin, the immaculate Mother of God, and the holy angels who serve her as Queen enfold all these dear ones with the protection of their prayers. *Angelis Deus mandavit de vobis, ut custodiant vos in omnibus viis vestris.*

I thank Penguin Random House for permission to include quotations from the following works: *The Comedy of Dante Alighieri the Florentine: Cantica I, Hell (L'Inferno)*, translated by Dorothy L. Sayers (Harmondsworth: Penguin, 1949); *The Comedy of Dante Alighieri the Florentine: Cantica II, Purgatory (Il Purgatorio)*, translated by Dorothy L. Sayers (Harmondsworth: Penguin, 1955); *The Comedy of Dante Alighieri the Florentine: Cantica III, Paradise (Il Paradiso)*, translated by Dorothy L. Sayers and Barbara Reynolds (London: Penguin, 1962); Dante, *Purgatory*, translated, edited, and with an introduction by Anthony Esolen (New York: The Modern Library, 1996); Dante, *Paradise*, translated, edited, and with an introduction by Anthony Esolen (New York: The Modern Library, 2007).

The Feast of Our Lady of Fatima
May 13, 2022

ABBREVIATIONS

AAS	*Acta apostolicae sedis*
Bonino	Serge-Thomas Bonino OP, *Les anges et les démons: Quatorze leçons de théologie* (Paris: Parole et Silence, 2007)
CCC	*The Catechism of the Catholic Church*
CCCM	*Corpus christianorum continuatio mediaevalis* (Turnhout: Brepols, 1966ff)
DCOO	*Doctoris ecstatici D. Dionysii Cartusiani opera omnia, cura et labore monachorum sacri Ordinis Cartusiensis* (Typis Cartusiae S.M. de Pratis, 1896-1935)
Divine Liturgy	*The Divine Liturgy of Our Father Among the Saints, John Chrysostom: The Greek Text together with a Translation into English* (Oxford: Oxford University Press, 1995)
DS	H. Denzinger and A. Schönmetzer SJ (eds.), *Enchiridion symbolorum definitionum et declarationum de rebus fidei et morum*, edition xxxiii (Barcelona & Freiburg im Breisgau: Herder, 1965)
Esolen	*The Divine Comedy: Purgatory [Purgatorio]* and *Paradise [Paradiso]*, translated by Anthony Esolen (New York: The Modern Library, 2004 & 2007)
PG	J. P. Migne (ed.), *Patrologia Graeca*
PL	J. P. Migne (ed.), *Patrologia Latina*
Sayers	*The Divine Comedy I & II: Hell [Inferno]* and *Purgatory [Purgatorio]*, translated by Dorothy L. Sayers (Harmondsworth: Penguin, 1949 & 1955)
Sayers-Reynolds	*The Divine Comedy III: Paradise [Paradiso]*, translated by Dorothy L. Sayers and Barbara Reynolds (London: Penguin, 1962)
SCG	St Thomas Aquinas, *Summa contra gentiles*
Sent.	St Thomas Aquinas, *Scriptum super libros Sententiarum*
ST	St Thomas Aquinas, *Summa theologiae*
Vonier, *Teaching*	Abbot Anscar Vonier OSB, "The Angels," in *The Teaching of the Catholic Church*, 2nd edition (London: Burns, Oates & Washbourne, 1951), 248–85

O world invisible, we view thee,
O world intangible, we touch thee,
O world unknowable, we know thee,
Inapprehensible, we clutch thee!

Does the fish soar to find the ocean,
The eagle plunge to find the air —
That we ask of the stars in motion
If they have rumor of thee there?

Not where the wheeling systems darken,
And our benumbed conceiving soars! —
The drift of pinions, would we hearken,
Beats at our own clay-shuttered doors.

The angels keep their ancient places; —
Turn but a stone, and start a wing!
'Tis ye, 'tis your enstrangèd faces,
That miss the many-splendored thing.

But (when so sad thou canst not sadder)
Cry; — and upon thy so sore loss
Shall shine the traffic of Jacob's ladder
Pitched betwixt Heaven and Charing Cross.

Yea, in the night, my Soul, my daughter,
Cry, — clinging to Heaven by the hems;
And lo, Christ walking on the water,
Not of Gennesareth, but Thames![1]

---

1   "The Kingdom of God: In No Strange Land," *Poems of Francis Thompson*, ed. Terence L. Connolly, SJ (New York & London: The Century Company, 1932), 293.

INTRODUCTION

E VEN IN HIS DARKEST HOURS, THE MAN who wrote the lines on the facing page had glimpses of glory. Between 1886 and 1888, Francis Thompson, ex-seminarian and failed medical student, was taking laudanum and sleeping rough. Yet, amidst the many dangers of his life, this strange poet of the London streets believed he was sheltered by God's holy angels; he was sure they were not oblivious of human infirmity, even if men were blind to angelic majesty. With hope, therefore, he could cry out, and *the traffic of Jacob's ladder*, the holy angels ascending in worship of God and descending in compassion for men, would bring him the comfort of *Christ walking on the water, not of Gennesareth, but Thames.*

Most people these days do not expect to *start wings* from underneath stones. Not just the atheists, who hold that material things are all there is, but even some claiming the name of Christian *miss the many-splendored thing*. The angels, they would say, are the product of a pre-scientific imagination, and therefore fit subjects for "demythologization,"[2] the cruel and unusual punishment reserved by Biblical critics for anything in Scripture at odds with what they take to be the modern outlook. What follows is a response to this skepticism. *World Invisible* is intended to help the Christian reader rediscover the reality of the angels, what they are and what they do, as understood by the Catholic Church and her Doctors.

'Tis ye, 'tis your enstrangèd faces,/ That miss the many-splendored thing. The Christian of today needs to feel the force of words

---

2   The terms "demythologize" and "demythologization," first used in English in the 1950s according to the OED, are associated principally with the liberal Protestant Rudolf Bultmann. "We cannot use electric lights and radios [says Bultmann] and, in the event of illness, avail ourselves of modern medical and clinical means and at the same time believe in the spirit and wonder world of the New Testament" (*New Testament and Mythology and Other Basic Writings* [Philadelphia: Fortress, 1984], 4).

uttered by the seventh-century English bishop St Cuthbert when he was still a shepherd boy on the border hills. As he watched his flock by night, he had a vision of angels carrying the soul of St Aidan of Lindisfarne into heaven and cried out, "Alas for us poor wretches, given over to sleep and sloth, we are not worthy to gaze on the light of the ever-watchful ministers of God."[3] As for us, poor wretches of the twenty-first century, we have fallen into the obtuseness of mind that William Blake condemned as "single vision and Newton's sleep."[4] Gratitude to modern science for the conveniences and cures it supplies lulls us into unawareness of the limitations of what Jacques Maritain called its "empiriometric" methodology (the business of measuring and observing) and of its lack of grounding in philosophical realism, even the realism of every man that is common sense.[5] The materialist, who "resolves all concepts into the measurable,"[6] will never understand that a spiritual soul informs the material body of man, still less that above and beyond humanity are angels, forms without matter, or that transcending everything bodily and all created spirits is He Who Is, the almighty and eternal God who is Spirit, the maker of all things, visible and invisible. "When you turn the world into a huge and meaningless machine, which man uses at the behest of his passions, you destroy, not only *de facto* but *de iure*, his ordering to true beatitude and the possibility of his knowing the universe and thereby ascending from the sensible world to the world of spirits."[7]

We must wake up from the sleep, with its nightmares, of "scientism," that idolizing of science which is the destruction of

---

3   *Vita S. Cudbercti*, cap. 4; *Venerabilis Bedae opera historica minora* (London: 1841), 56.

4   "Now I a fourfold vision see,/ And a fourfold vision is given to me;/ 'Tis fourfold in my supreme delight/ And threefold in soft Beulah's night/ And twofold Always. May God us keep/ From Single vision & Newton's sleep." Letter to Thomas Butts, November 22, 1802; *William Blake: Complete Writings with Variant Readings*, edited by Geoffrey Keynes (Oxford: Oxford University Press, 1972), 818.

5   Cf. "Réalisme et sens commun," in Jacques Maritain, *Distinguer pour unir ou Les degrés du savoir*, new edition (Paris: Desclée de Brouwer, 1932), 158–63.

6   Maritain, *Les degrés du savoir*, 270.

7   J.-M. Vernier, *Les anges chez St Thomas d'Aquin: Fondements historiques et principes philosophiques* (Paris: Nouvelles éditions latines, 1986), 135.

science, and, heeding the challenge of St Cuthbert, raise up our minds to "the watchful ministers of God." There is infinite perfection in God Himself, and even in the finite universe that He made is richness beyond measure. "Belief in angels," argues the novelist Martin Mosebach, "says simply that the entire cosmos is filled to the brim with divine reality."[8] The last star on the final frontier of the most remote of the galaxies is under the stewardship and supervision of the angels of God. Our lives, too, are steeped in the influences of created persons higher in nature than we are. We have unseen companions above and around us. The blessed spirits bring to our souls from God the brightness of truth and the warmth of goodness, while hostile intelligences, fallen spiritual creatures, conspire to confuse us with their lies and dishearten us with their malevolence. No Christian cosmology can therefore be complete, no account of human life fully adequate, without reference to the angels, the good and the bad, the glorious and the reprobate.

THE ANGELIC DOCTOR

This book is an exposition of the Catholic doctrine of the angels conducted under the tutelage of St Thomas Aquinas. He is the Doctor whom the Church calls "Angelic" and commends to students of theology as their first teacher under God and her own Magisterium. His treatise on the angels in the First Part of the *Summa Theologiae* demands our attention as the most comprehensive and rigorous study of the subject in the Tradition. It is not a devotional digression from the main arguments of the *Summa*; on the contrary, as Thomas Chrysostom O'Brien said, it "contains some of the clearest and profoundest statements of his most distinctive teachings; it is in truth a *summa* within the *Summa*."[9] St Thomas has much to teach us about the angels and, through the study of the angels, about the chief mysteries of the Catholic faith.

8   Martin Mosebach, *The Heresy of Formlessness: The Roman Liturgy and Its Enemy*, revised and expanded ed. (Brooklyn: Angelico, 2018), 110.
9   T. C. O'Brien, Introduction, *St Thomas Aquinas: Summa Theologiae*, vol. 14, Divine Government (1a 103–109) (London: Eyre & Spottiswoode, 1975), x.

Friar Thomas of Aquino understood the angels as well as any human being can in this life, and in certain ways he resembled them. He was a man of flesh and blood, yet, says his early-fourteenth-century biographer Bernardo Gui, he seemed able in prayer "to raise his mind to God as if the body's burden did not exist for him."[10] Sometimes when praying, his body was lifted heavenward from the ground.[11] The starting-point of his intellectual knowledge was what he perceived through his senses, and to the images of sense-experience he had constantly to return. He thought, as all men think, by discursive reason, arriving at conclusions by argument and after study. However, the penetration and swiftness of his understanding, chiefly dependent, as he always insisted, on prayer,[12] was reminiscent of the way in which the angels know.[13] His chastity, too, was angelic: after he had driven a harlot from his room with a burning log, angels came to guard his virginity.[14] By God's grace, his whole life was so free from grave sin that Brother Reginald, who heard his last confession, said he always "found him like a little child for purity."[15] "O happy wayfarer through this world [says Gui], who won on earth the citizenship of Heaven, and through chastity the company of the angels."[16]

In view of St Thomas's affinity with the angels in prayerfulness, intelligence, and chastity, it is not surprising to find that his writings on the angels are so well developed. He loved to contemplate the angels and pass on to others the fruits of his

---

10   *The Life of St Thomas Aquinas: Biographical Documents*, trans. and ed. with an introduction by Kenelm Foster, OP (London: Longmans, 1959), 36f.
11   Ibid., 42.
12   Ibid., 37.
13   See pp. 69–72 below.
14   *The Life of St Thomas Aquinas*, 30. "If, however, we seek to discover the peculiar and specific characteristics of his sanctity, there occurs to us in the first place that virtue which gives Thomas a certain likeness to the angelic natures, and that is chastity; he preserved it unsullied in a crisis of the most pressing danger and was therefore considered worthy to be girded by the angels with a mystic cincture." Pope Pius XI, *Studiorum ducem* (1923), n. 4.
15   Ibid., 57.
16   Ibid., 31.

contemplation. "If St Thomas's mind was suffused with the light of his insights into God's fontal goodness," says Father O'Brien, "it was also a mind teeming with angels."[17] It is therefore right and just that Tradition should honor Friar Thomas of Aquino with the title "angelic." The Preface of St Thomas Aquinas in the traditional Dominican Missal praises him as "an angel in purity of life and elevation of mind."[18]

Angel-like in his virtues, St Thomas is entirely free from "angelism" in his thinking, that is, the false spiritualizing of man's nature and supernatural perfection. On the contrary, in both his philosophy and his theology, as Josef Pieper puts it, we find an "unabashed affirmation of the body."[19] Although the image of God in man lies chiefly in his rational soul, St Thomas insists that "the soul united with the body is more like God than the soul separated from the body is, because it possesses its nature in more complete fashion."[20] The soul on its own is no more a human person than the hand or foot on its own is a person.[21] St Thomas is always respectful of the Fathers, even when he disagrees with them, but his impatience is evident when he describes as "unreasonable" the claim of some theologians of the early centuries that in the state of innocence the increase of mankind would have taken place without intercourse, just as the angels are multiplied by the operation of divine power.[22] By contrast, St Thomas argues that not only would the bodies of man and woman have been united in the task of procreation, their purity and the greater sensitivity of their bodies would have made the

---

17   T. C. O'Brien, Introduction, *St Thomas Aquinas: Summa Theologiae*, vol. 14, Divine Government (1a 103–109) (London: Eyre & Spottiswoode, 1975), xvi.

18   *The St Dominic Missal: Latin-English* (New York: St Dominic Missal, 1959), 659.

19   Josef Pieper, *Guide to Thomas Aquinas* (New York: Pantheon, 1962), vii.

20   *De potentia* q. 5, a. 10, ad 5.

21   "The hypostasis or person is not just any particular substance, but that which has the complete nature of the species. Hence a hand, or a foot, cannot be called a hypostasis or person, nor is the soul, since it is a part of the human species" (*ST* 1a q. 75, a. 4, ad 2).

22   St Thomas mentions St Gregory of Nyssa as one who held this unreasonable opinion (cf. *ST* 1a q. 98, a. 2).

pleasure of the conjugal act more intense than it is now for their fallen offspring.[23] Absolutely speaking, says Thomas, man is less perfectly in God's image than the angels are, because the angels have more perfect intellects. But certain aspects of his bodiliness make man more like God than the angels could ever be: procreation, a human being begetting another human being, is a kind of image of the begetting of God the Son by God the Father, and, just as God is everywhere in the world, so the whole human soul exists in the whole human body and its every part.[24]

THE ANGELIC LIFE AND THEOLOGY OF MONKS

No Anglophone theologian of the twentieth century gave more attention to the angels than Dom Anscar Vonier, abbot and rebuilder of Buckfast.[25] In a little book published in 1928, he expounded the Catholic and Thomistic doctrine of the angels with simplicity and a dash of humor. His insights are a major source for what is said in these pages.

It is fitting to draw upon the wisdom of a monastic theologian in a book on the angels, because, from its beginnings in the early centuries of the Church, the monastic life has been seen as a foretaste of heaven, and for that very reason as an angelic life, for the angels fill the heavens. According to St Hildegard of Bingen, "even in their clothing, with great humility, they imitate the angelic order."[26] The habit is heavenly: the fact that it is different from earthly dress is a sign that the monk or nun seeks citizenship, not here below, but in "the city of the living God" and "the company of many thousands of angels" (Heb 12:22). That is why, according to Dom Jean Leclercq, in the monastic centuries, "to recall a monk to the practice of his obligations, it was enough to tell him he was wearing the vesture of the angels."[27]

---

23   *ST* 1a q. 98, a. 2, ad 3.
24   Cf. *ST* 1a q. 93, a. 3.
25   See Ernest Graf, OSB, *Anscar Vonier: Abbot of Buckfast* (London: Burns & Oates, 1957).
26   St Hildegard, *Scivias* pars 3, visio 12, cap. 8; CCCM 43A.610.
27   Dom Jean Leclercq, OSB, *La vie parfaite: Points de vue sur l'essence de l'état religieux* (Turnhout & Paris: Brepols, 1948), 21. The discarding of the

The monastic life is angelic because monks and nuns are called to imitate, within the limits of human frailty, the blessed spirits' perpetual praise of God. The holy angels serve and worship the holy and undivided Trinity in the clarity of vision, whereas monks and nuns serve and worship the Triune God in the obscurity of faith. Yet when, with the eyes of faith and love, they contemplate the Trinity and the human face of the incarnate Son, and offer the divine majesty the complete surrender of their bodies and souls, they have a foretaste of the essential acts of heavenly beatitude.

The life of monks and nuns is angelic, because it detaches them from those merely earthly goods that tend to slow the Christian down in pursuing perfect charity. The only bridegroom of the consecrated virgin is the Lord Jesus, the incarnate Word and Redeemer; the only fatherhood of the monk is spiritual; the priest-monk loves and serves the Church, Christ's Bride, with a heart undivided and undistracted by earthly love. The treasures of the poor men and women who follow the poor Christ are stored up for them by the angels in heaven, where neither moth nor rust can destroy (cf. Mt 6:19). The liberty of those vowed to obedience is liberation from self-will, for "to know God is to live, to serve Him is to reign."[28] "In my opinion," says St Bernard, "because of the perfect renunciation of the world it requires, and because of the singularly exalted spiritual life it fosters, and by which it stands high above all other forms of life, it makes those

---

habit in recent decades is a product of angelism. Although every Christian hopes to join the angels in glory, and the monk strives to imitate the angels in certain respects, no monk, no man, can pretend to apprehend reality by an entirely spiritual intuition, as the pure spirits do. Human beings attain understanding through a humble process that starts off with the data of sense-knowledge. They cannot, therefore, be expected to know by intuition or mystical perception that someone is a monk or nun; they need outward signs that this or that person is consecrated to the perfection of charity by the observance of a rule. The senses and the mind of the ordinary Catholic require such prompts, and so do the senses and the minds of the monks themselves: the differentness of their dress brings home to them daily that they desire to perfect, by the total gift of self, the clothing with Christ that took place in their baptism (cf. Gal 3:27).

28   St Gregory the Great, *Liber sacramentorum, Missa pro pace, Ad complendum*; PL 78.206A.

who profess it, and love it, like the angels and different from men. It re-establishes the image of God in a man and configures him to Christ in the manner of Baptism."[29]

As noted earlier, it is especially in their virginity, or perpetual and perfect continence, that consecrated persons resemble the angels. Our Lord teaches us that after our resurrection we shall neither marry nor be married, but "shall be as the angels of God in heaven" (Mt 22:30). We shall be raised in our own naturally human bodies, with their proper sexual identity,[30] but the task of procreation will be at an end, all our desires will be at peace, and we shall be like the angels in their freedom from the disordered passions of the flesh.[31] Those, then, who even now make the total gift of themselves to God without bodily union with an earthly spouse anticipate the resurrection and live an angel-like life. In his encyclical *Sacra virginitas*, Pope Pius XII says that virginity "fully deserves the name of angelic virtue," and invokes the testimony of St Cyprian writing to virgins: "What we are to be, you have already begun to be. You already possess in this world the glory of the resurrection; you pass through the world without suffering its contagion. In preserving virginal chastity, you are the equals of the angels of God."[32]

Byzantine iconography represents St John the Baptist, model for all monks, with angels' wings. The reason is, first, St John's fulfillment of the office of an angel, that is, of a *messenger* sent by God. In the words of the prophet Malachi, quoted by our Lord: "Behold, I send my angel ['my messenger'] before thy face, who shall prepare thy way before thee" (Lk 7:27; cf. Mal 3:1). The second reason is the Baptist's resemblance to the angels in the heroism of his asceticism, later imitated by the Desert Fathers and the hermits of every age. An anonymous medieval author sees hermits as the special kinsmen of the angels: "They hide themselves

29   St Bernard of Clairvaux, De praecepto et dispensatione cap. 17, n. 54; PL 182.889.
30   Cf. St Thomas Aquinas, Sent. lib. 4, d. 44, q. 1, a. 3, qc. 3.
31   Cf. Pope John Paul II, Vita consecrata (March 25, 1996), n. 32.
32   Pope Pius XII, Sacra virginitas (March 25, 1954), n. 29, citing St Cyprian, De habitu virginum, 4; PL 4.443.

in mountain caves and the hollows of the valleys, in order to have fellowship with the angelic spirits. They are enraptured in contemplation of the richness of glory, and in the flesh, forgetful of the flesh, they weary their nature by constant meditation."[33]

THE POET OF THE ANGELS AND HIS ILLUSTRATOR

The starting-point for each chapter of this book will be a text from the greatest of all Christian poems: the *Divine Comedy* of Dante Alighieri. It has much to say about the angels in the nine fiery circles of their orders,[34] and bears the imprint of a mind formed by the reading of the Angelic Doctor.[35] Writes Romano Guardini:

> Angels enfold Dante's destiny with a solicitude that is at first barely discernible, but becomes ever clearer. The solicitude is not based on a personal connection with this particular man, of the kind that Virgil and Beatrice have with him; for the angels, he represents a part of the great destiny of mankind as a whole. The angels' attentiveness is aimed at bringing to completion the Kingdom of God, in which Dante has an important place.[36]

The first encounter with an angel is in the ninth canto of the *Inferno*. A clap of thunder greets the arrival of a holy angel, who opens the gates of Dis and rebukes the demons, the "outcasts of Heaven, despicable crew."[37] In relation to Hell, the blessed spirits

---

33 *Sermo 69, In dedicatione ecclesiae* 1; PL 144.901D–902A.
34 Cf. *Paradiso* 28, 25ff.
35 In his encyclical on the sixth centenary of Dante's death, Pope Benedict XV says that Dante "especially followed Thomas Aquinas, prince of the schools" (*In praeclara summorum*, n. 4). But Dante should not be called a Thomist. "Since the pioneering labors of Bruno Nardi and [Étienne] Gilson's brilliant book [*Dante et la philosophie*], it has become increasingly evident that Dante cannot be called a Thomist in any strict sense as denoting a body of doctrine characteristic of St Thomas.... Nevertheless Gilson was plainly right to say that Dante [a] *profondément admiré et aimé saint Thomas*" Kenelm Foster, OP, "St Thomas and Dante," in *The Two Dantes and Other Studies* (London: Darton, Longman & Todd, 1977), 56, 61.
36 Romano Guardini, *Engel: Theologische Betrachtungen* (Mainz: Matthias-Grünewald-Verlag, 1995), 20.
37 Cf. *Inferno* 9, 91; Sayers, 125.

are the ministers of God's justice and wrath. In the *Purgatorio* the holy angels have a higher profile. As Dante and Virgil approach the gates of purgatory, they meet an angel on guard duty. With a flashing sword, he marks Dante's forehead with seven P's representing the deadly sins and instructs him to wash the wounds away in purgatory.[38] There are seven cornices on Mount Purgatory for the purging of the remains of the seven sins. At each level there is a penance, a meditation, a prayer, a blessing, and an assisting angel. In the Earthly Paradise, scattering flowers and chanting verses from Scripture and the *Aeneid*, angels acclaim the arrival of Beatrice: "These angels [to quote Guardini again] are an overflow from the fullness of Heaven. They urge the pilgrim, who has climbed so high, to press onward toward Heaven; he is enveloped in their devotion and love."[39] Finally, in the twenty-eighth and twenty-ninth cantos of the *Paradiso*, Beatrice speaks to Dante of the nine orders of the angels in their celestial glory. The contemplation of the angelic hierarchies is Dante's preparation for seeing the Queen of the Angels, Blessed Mary Ever-Virgin, the glorified humanity of the only-begotten Son, and the eternal light of the Creator of the angels and all things, the Holy and Undivided Trinity.

Accompanying Dante's words will be illustrations of the *Commedia* made by Sandro Botticelli to a commission from Lorenzo de' Medici. The drawings are well suited to our purposes for two reasons. First, as Sir Kenneth Clark says, they have "qualities that are essentially Dantesque: purity and economy."[40] These qualities are also in a certain way angelic, for the angels are pure and operate with that economy which metaphysics calls simplicity. Secondly, the man whose drawings "realize with miraculous fullness as much of [Dante's] poem as art can express"[41] was a convert to the thinking of Fra Girolamo Savonarola, through whom he

38 Cf. *Purgatorio* 9, 82, 113–14.
39 Guardini, *Engel*, 72. See *Purgatorio* 30.
40 Kenneth Clark, *The Drawings by Sandro Botticelli for Dante's* Divine Comedy: *After the Originals in the Berlin Museums and the Vatican* (London: Thames & Hudson, 1976), 24.
41 Ronald Lightbown, *Botticelli: Life and Work* (London: Thames & Hudson, 1989), 294.

doubtless assimilated much of the doctrine of St Thomas, the Angelic Doctor.[42]

ANGELS AND EVERYMAN

There are three reasons for Christians to take an interest in the angels. The first concerns the worship of God, the second our understanding of human nature, and the third our hope for eternal life.

First, the study of the angels should move us to more fervent praise of almighty God. They are closer to God, just as matter is closer to nothing.[43] Therefore, the wonder we feel at the thought of what the angels are and do should make us approach their Creator with renewed humility, reverence, and admiration. As it was for Isaiah, on seeing the Seraphim, and for St John, when he heard the voice of many angels, so should it be for us: thinking about the angels of God ought to move us to the adoration of God (cf. Is 6:5; Apoc 5:13). The honoring of the angels redounds to the greater glory of God, One and Triune.

Secondly, thinking about the angels helps man see himself in perspective. It humbles his pride. Of all the intellects created by God, the human is the feeblest, a snail by comparison with the eagle mind of the angel. Yet angelology also gives us cause for wonder at the vocation God has given man, "made a little less than the angels" (cf. Ps 8:6), to be a microcosm and mixture of the high and the low in God's creation, "to the ancestral clod kin, and to cherubin,"[44] and to serve as a mediator for the joining

---

42   Although he condemned the reading of Dante in churches, Savonarola shared the poet's thirst for a renewal of the Church and his loathing for simony. "As it becomes Dantesque, the art of Botticelli assumes a Savonarolan posture." Michel Feuillet, *Botticelli et Savonarole: L'humanisme à l'épreuve du feu* (Paris: Cerf, 2010), 82.

43   Cf. St Augustine, *Confessions* 12, ch. 7, n. 7; PL 32.828.

44   "Great arm-fellow of God!/ To the ancestral clod/ Kin,/ And to cherubin" ("Any Saint," *Poems of Francis Thompson*, 183). "As image of God, man is lord of creation and 'microcosm.' This second concept, which was widely used in Platonism and Stoicism, was adopted by the Cappadocian Fathers and given a Christian dimension: man is a 'microcosm' because (1) he unites, in his hypostatic existence, the intelligible and sensible aspects of creation; (2) he is given by God the *task* and function to make this unity ever more

of the extremes.[45] Thus, in assuming the nature of man in the Virgin's womb, God the Son recapitulates all things in Himself.

> Since man is composed of a nature that is spiritual as well as bodily, occupying a kind of borderland between the two natures, what is done for man's salvation [says St Thomas] concerns the whole of creation. For lower, bodily creatures seem to be set aside for man's use and are somehow subject to him. But the higher, spiritual creature, namely the angelic, has in common with man the attainment of a final end.... And so it seems fitting that the universal cause of all things should assume into the unity of person that [human nature] in which He shares more completely with all creatures.[46]

Contemplation of the angels, and of our likeness to them in soul, guards us from materialism, but consideration of our unlikeness to them in our bodies, and in the composite unity of our nature, protects us from Cartesian dualism and angelistic delusion. We are neither apes nor angels, nor ghosts in machines, but men, the sons of Adam, and to be men we must have body as well as soul.

We are human beings, not angels, and to forget the truth of that truism is as dangerous as it is ridiculous. As Pascal said, "man is neither angel nor beast, and unhappily he who wants to act the angel acts the beast (*qui veut faire l'ange fait la bête*)."[47] Only the fallen angel, who despises our bodily nature, could lead a man into angelism; from such spiritual pride springs contempt for human infirmity and for those stages of human life in which a man is most dependent on others: infancy, mortal illness, and

---

perfect, especially after the Fall, when forces of disintegration and division are also actively at work in creation" (John Meyendorff, *Byzantine Theology* [London & Oxford: Mowbray, 1974], 142).

45 "The power of the Divine Creator was manifested in man's body when its matter was produced by creation. But it was fitting that the human body should be made of the four elements, that man might have something in common with the inferior bodies, as a kind of mediator [*medium*] between spiritual and corporeal substances." *ST* 1a q. 91, a. 1, ad 1.

46 *SCG*, lib. 4, cap. 55, n. 3.

47 Blaise Pascal, *Pensées*, n. 358 (London & Paris: Dent & Crés, 1913), 150.

old age. One would-be angel, the Desert Father John the Dwarf, learnt his lesson the hard way:

> One day he said to his elder brother, "I should like to be free of all care, like the angels, who do not work, but ceaselessly offer worship to God." So he took off his cloak and went away into the desert. After a week he came back to his brother. When he knocked on the door, he heard his brother say, before he opened it, "Who are you?" He said, "I am John, your brother." But he replied, "John has become an angel, and henceforth he is no longer among men." Then the other begged him saying, "It is I." However, his brother did not let him in, but left him there in distress until morning. Then, opening the door, he said to him, "You are a man and you must once again work in order to eat." Then John made a prostration before him, saying, "Forgive me."[48]

In the early eleventh century St Fulbert of Chartres sums up John's return to humanity and sanity in four crisp lines of verse:

> Cured of his folly, he'll let him
> An angel be who can,
> Himself he finds it hard enough
> To be a decent man.[49]

The doctrine of the angels also sheds light on the sufferings and struggles of human life. We are *fallen* creatures. Our nature has been wounded by the sin of our first father, Adam. Now we cannot understand that sin and its effects on us without reference to the very first sinner, the fallen angel, at whose instigation Adam sinned and disobeyed God, and who still prowls around, seeking whom he may devour. The devil is tireless in tempting us to join him in his insurrection against God, and, ultimately, to keep him company in eternal torment. If we do not believe there are such

48 *The Sayings of the Desert Fathers: The Alphabetic Collection*, ed. and trans. Benedicta Ward, SLG (London & Oxford: Mowbray, 1981), 86.
49 St Fulbert of Chartres, *De Johanne abbate*, ed. and trans. by Helen Waddell in her *More Latin Lyrics: From Virgil to Milton* (London: Gollancz, 1980), 233.

things as angels, then we cannot believe in fallen angels, in which case Lucifer can get on with his scheming without being noticed. Even worse, if we deny the existence of angels but insist on believing in a superhuman power of evil, we fall into the trap of the Manichees and imagine Satan to be an uncreated rival to God.

Thirdly, we need to know something about the holy angels, because, in His loving wisdom, God has called us to share their happiness in heaven. This is the teaching of our Lord himself, when He says that "the children of the resurrection" will be "equal to the angels" (cf. Lk 20:36). The Apostle Paul likewise lifts up our Christian hope towards "the heavenly Jerusalem and... the company of many thousands of angels" (Heb 12:22). The Father of mercies has destined us, through the Precious Blood of the Son and the fire of the Holy Spirit, to be taken up into the orders of the angels, and to fill the gaps left by the apostate angels. We cannot rank with the pure spirits in nature, but, as St Thomas teaches us, by God's generosity (*ex liberalitate Dei*) and through the gift of His grace, we "can merit such glory that we become the angels' equals in their divers grades."[50] Thus, as Abbot Vonier puts it, "the elect of the human race will be not only the outside fringe of the spirit world; they will, on the contrary, be shining stars in every one of the spirit planes."[51] Now, since the angels are pure spirits, simple intelligences, the only way we can join them in fellowship is by knowledge, and by the love that follows from knowledge. Divine wisdom and mercy have destined us to share with the angels not only the supreme supernatural knowledge that is the clear vision of the Blessed Trinity, but also their elevated natural mode of knowing.[52]

---

50   *ST* 1a q. 108, a. 8.

51   Vonier, *Teaching*, 283.

52   After death the soul, whatever its state, has a natural knowledge derived from God, the Father of lights: "The separated soul does not understand through innate species [writes St Thomas], nor through species abstracted thence, nor through species it retains.... No, the soul in that state understands through participated species derived from the influence of the divine light, in which it participates, like the other separate substances, though in a lesser degree. Hence, as soon as it ceases to act by turning to the body, the soul turns at once to the higher things. This knowledge is natural, for

According to St John Henry Newman, God reveals the existence of the angels to us, at least in part, so that "Heaven may be as little as possible an unknown place in our imaginations."[53] In *The Dream of Gerontius* he suggests that the angels make up the very fabric of the Father's house:

> The smallest portions of this edifice,
> Cornice, or frieze, or balustrade, or stair,
> The very pavement is made up of life —
> Of holy, blessed, and immortal beings,
> Who hymn their Maker's praise continually.[54]

"The reality of a glorified angelic world," says the French Dominican Fr Bonino, "shows us that the Kingdom of God is not a utopia. It is the Kingdom of Heaven, a kingdom already in actuality, a glory created by God, not so much to be built as to be welcomed by man."[55]

INVISIBLE WORLD, REAL AND CLOSE:
THE PLAN AND PURPOSE OF THIS BOOK

Six days before his death in 1958, the Venerable Pope Pius XII addressed an audience of pilgrims from the United States. On their journey to Rome they had seen much of the beauty of this visible world, but he invited them to raise their minds, as he was raising his in those last days of his life, to the invisible world of God's angels in the eternal city of Heaven. The words of this great pope express perfectly the purpose of this book. His prayer for his hearers is mine for my readers.

God is the author of the influence of both the light of grace and the light of nature" (*ST* 1a q. 89, a. 1, ad 3). "Equality with the angels must necessarily mean intellectual equality, as all the attributes of spirit are intellectual, or connected with the intellect. Thus it will be possible for the elect to converse with the angels in 'their own tongue'" (Anscar Vonier, OSB, "The Human Soul and the Angels of God," in *The Collected Works of Abbot Vonier*, vol. 3, *The Soul and the Spiritual Life* [London: Burns & Oates, 1953], 156).
53 "The Powers of Nature," in *Parochial and Plain Sermons*, vol. 2 (London, New York, etc.: Longmans, Green, & Co., 1908), 367.
54 "The Dream of Gerontius," in *Verses on Various Occasions* (London: Burns & Oates, Longmans, Green, & Co., 1903), 354.
55 Bonino, 108.

You have come a long and tortuous way to Rome, fond mother of your souls. Over ocean and inland sea, with visits to cities of men and shrines rich with sacred memories, you have already seen much of this world. And your travels are not yet over. Earth and sky, hills and valleys, the capital cities of different nations with their ancient monuments and modern inhabitants: your eyes have feasted on them all. And when mysterious night, stealing over the shoreless sea, drew back the dazzling curtain from across the sky, creation widened on your view, as the heavenly host of stars and planets came out to reflect the glory of their Creator. What a vast and beautiful world, you reflected, this visible world!

But October is a month that checks the vision for a moment, reminding one's inner spirit that there is another world, an invisible world, yet as real as the one you see and quite as close to you. Yesterday the Church celebrated the feast of the Holy Angels. They are inhabitants of this invisible world that is all around you. They were in the cities you visited as guardians of God's providence; they have accompanied you on your journey. Did not Christ say of the little children, who were always so dear to his pure and loving heart: "Their angels in heaven are always looking on the face of my Father who is in heaven" (Mt 18:10)? And when the children passed on to youth, and then to adult life, did their Angels desert them? No, indeed! "The guardians of our race,/ Our angel guides we hail;/ Our Father sendeth forth to aid our nature frail/ These heavenly friends, lest we should suffer overthrow/ Through cunning of our subtle foe."[56] This same thought recurs again and again in the writings of the Fathers of the Church. No one is so humble, but he has angels to attend him. They are so glorious, so pure, so wonderful, yet they are given to be your companions, charged to watch carefully over you, lest you fall away from Christ, their Lord. Not only do they wish to defend you against

---

56   Hymn at Vespers of the Feast of the Holy Guardian Angels; see *The Monastic Diurnal or The Day Hours of the Monastic Breviary in Latin and English* (Farnborough: St Michael's Abbey Press, 2004), 295.

dangers lurking along the way; they are also active at your side with a word of encouragement to your souls, as you strive to ascend higher and higher to closeness to God through Christ.

Dearly beloved pilgrims, receiving you at the beginning of this month of October, we could not refrain from leaving with you a brief word of paternal exhortation to awaken and sharpen your realization of the invisible world about you—"for the things that are seen last for a moment, the things that are not seen are eternal" (2 Cor 4:18)—and to foster a certain familiar acquaintance with the angels, who are so constant in their solicitude for your salvation and holiness. You will spend, God grant it, an eternity of joy with them; begin to know them now.... May the angels carry our prayer for you before the throne of God, and through the intercession of their glorious Queen be the bearers to you of countless graces from your divine Savior.[57]

---

57 To pilgrims from various diocese of the United States (October 3, 1958).

BOTTICELLI, PARADISO 28

1

NINE · FIERY · RINGS

THE EXISTENCE OF THE ANGELS

I saw a point that shot out rays of light
    so keen, you have to shut your eyes before
    the searing brightness of its radiant might....

About so near the point a fiery ring
    revolved so rapidly it would defeat
    the swiftest girdling of the universe.

And this was girdled by a second ring,
    that by a third, the third then by ring four,
    and likewise four by five, and five by six.

As for the following seventh's vast domain,
    only if Iris' bow were fully drawn
    could it embrace it with the tightest strain.

So too for eight and nine, and each ring spun
    more slowly than the ring that came before,
    according to their distance from the One;

And the least distant from the purest fire
    shone with the clearest flame, I think because
    the point entruthed itself (*s'invera*) most fully there.[1]

BEATRICE "IMPARADISES" DANTE'S mind: she informs his every thought with the beauty of heaven.[2] As he looks into her eyes, he sees in reflection a point of light of piercing brightness and, whirling round

---

1   *Paradiso* 28, 16–18; Esolen, 297.
2   ...*che 'mparadisa la mia mente* (*Paradiso*, canto 28, line 3). Sayers-Reynolds renders this untranslatable phrase as "who fills with Paradise my mind" (301).

it, nine shining rings. The point represents the simplicity of the Triune God, "whence Heaven and all things depend";[3] the rings are the blessed spirits in hierarchies of a more and more perfect seeing of God and an ever greater likeness to Him.

In his drawing of Canto 28, Botticelli shows us not a sharply stabbed point but a lightly sketched circle, with, on the right side of the page, the name *trinit[à]*, "Trinity." Dancing underneath are the nine orders of the angels, each with its own emblem: Angels with small tablets, Archangels holding scrolls, Principalities robed in priestly stoles, Powers bearing orbs and scepters, Virtues wielding crusader shields, Dominations waving cross-emblazoned flags, Thrones shaking tambourines. The Cherubim and Seraphim, the highest of the angels and the closest of them all to their Creator, the Blessed Trinity, defy the artist's charcoal, and appear as faintly traced rings of winged heads.

Dante is not surprised to find the noble spirits in heaven, for their existence is a truth of the Faith and their function in the cosmic order the certain teaching of the Fathers. He knows, therefore, that when he reaches the Jerusalem above, myriads of angels will keep him company. In this chapter, like Dante, I shall take the existence of the angels for granted, or rather, as he did, accept it with faith as divinely revealed and proposed as such by the Church, and show that there is much to be learnt from the simple fact of the angels' existence, their hierarchical ordering, and their number beyond earthly ease of counting.

THE EXISTENCE OF THE ANGELS

Today, as in the past, there are errors about the angels to right and to left. The Sadducees of old (cf. Acts 23:8), followed by the Modernists and Liberal Protestants of our own times, deny there are such things as angels, while the New Age cults, like the heresies combated by the Apostle (cf. Col 2:18), are obsessed with angels to the point of idolatry. The popes of the last century defended the existence of the angels against the skepticism of the Modernists.

---

3   *Paradiso* 28, 42; Esolen, 298–99.

"Some," says Pope Pius XII, "even question whether angels are personal creatures, and whether matter differs essentially from spirit."[4] In July 1986 St John Paul II began a series of general audience addresses on the angels as part of his systematic exposition of the Catholic faith: "Our catecheses on God, the Creator of the world, cannot be concluded without paying adequate attention to a precise content of Divine Revelation: the creation of purely spiritual beings, which Sacred Scripture calls 'angels.'"[5] The *Catechism of the Catholic Church* makes this unambiguous declaration: "The existence of the spiritual, non-corporeal beings that Sacred Scripture usually calls 'angels' is a truth of faith. The witness of Scripture is as clear as the unanimity of Tradition."[6] Angels have no doubts about anything. If they did, then they would have more reason for doubting the existence of men, matter and spirit in an improbable mix, than men have for doubting there could be such beautifully logical creatures as the bodiless spirits.

The chief document of the Magisterium dealing with the angels is the *Definition* against the Manichees (the Albigensians and Cathars) promulgated by the Fourth Lateran Council in 1215.

> We firmly believe and simply confess that there is only one true God, eternal, immense and unchangeable, incomprehensible, omnipotent and ineffable, the Father and the Son and the Holy Spirit: Three Persons but One entirely simple Essence, Substance, or Nature. The Father is from no one, the Son from the Father alone, the Holy Spirit equally from both. Without beginning, always and without end, the Father begetting, the Son being born, and the Holy Spirit proceeding, consubstantial and coequal and co-omnipotent and coeternal, the one principle of the universe, the Creator of all things visible and invisible, spiritual and corporeal: by His almighty power, at once (*simul*) from the beginning of time, He made from nothing both kinds of creatures, the spiritual and the corporeal, namely, the angelic and the earthly

---

4   *Humani generis* (August 12, 1950); DS 3891.
5   Audience Address, July 9, 1986.
6   CCC 328.

(*mundanam*), and then the human creature, constituted alike, as it were, of spirit and body. For the devil and the other demons were indeed created by God naturally good but made themselves evil by their own doing. As for man, he sinned at the suggestion of the devil.[7]

The Council here defines the following points of doctrine as revealed truths to which we must give the assent of divine and Catholic faith. First, angels exist. Secondly, they are creatures of the one true God. Thirdly, the devil and his demons were created naturally good by God but became evil by their own doing. Fourthly, the first man sinned at the suggestion of the devil. To this list of defined dogmas, we should add the guardianship of the angels, which is an example of a divinely revealed truth that has come to us from Sacred Scripture and Sacred Tradition without any pope or council needing to define it by an extraordinary exercise of the Magisterium.[8] Throughout the centuries the Church has taught, on the foundation of Scripture and Tradition, that at least some of the angels serve as the guardians of men.[9] We can also deduce from the words of the Fourth Lateran Council that the angels are purely spiritual creatures, by contrast with man, who is bodily as well as spiritual, and that they were created by God "from the beginning of time," and at the same time as the temporal and bodily universe. If not strictly *de fide*, whether through the ordinary Magisterium or the extraordinary, these opinions are the general teaching of the masters of sacred doctrine, including St Thomas Aquinas.

7   The Fourth Council of the Lateran, *Definition against the Albigensians and Cathars* (1215); DS 800.
8   On the ordinary magisterium, see the Second Vatican Council's Dogmatic Constitution on the Church, *Lumen gentium*, n. 25.
9   Thirty years ago, the Congregation for the Doctrine of the Faith promulgated a decree correcting what seemed to be aberrant opinions in the angelology of the association Opus Angelorum: *Decretum de doctrina et usibus particularibus consociationis cui nomen* Opus angelorum (June 6, 1992). The members of the association responded positively and in a spirit of obedience to the decree, and in 2010 the Congregation reported that its members were "living loyally and serenely in conformity with the doctrine of the Church, and with canon law and liturgical law" (*Circular Letter to the Presidents of the Episcopal Conferences regarding the Association Opus Angelorum*, October 2, 2010).

ARGUING FOR SEPARATED SUBSTANCES:
THE ANGELS AND THE PHILOSOPHERS

God revealed the existence of the angels throughout the history of salvation, and as Catholics we give the assent of faith to that revealed truth. Nevertheless, in itself "the existence of the angels is not strictly a supernatural mystery, and so does not elude the capacities of natural reason."[10] Therefore, in principle, it is not beyond the wit of man to perceive that a complete universe ought to contain incorporeal creatures, and it is reasonable to conclude that such beings probably exist.[11]

The ancient Greek philosophers, without the benefit of divine revelation, concluded there were spiritual entities that were inferior to God but greater than man. In his late and incomplete work *On Separate Substances*, St Thomas Aquinas gives a systematic description of this philosophical angelology, deriving profit from whatever is in harmony with the Catholic faith, and refuting what is contrary to it. The occasion of writing seems to have been a feast of the holy angels, which he was unable to observe by devotion in choir but honored by study in his cell.

The first of the Greeks to philosophize on the nature of things, the pre-Socratics, believed that only bodies existed, and that therefore the first principles of things were corporeal elements: water (Thales), air (Diogenes), or fire (Heraclitus).[12] Moreover, since they held that the first principle should be regarded as a god, the early philosophers attributed divinity to these elements. There could be no substances without bodies: the only things that existed, therefore, were the "gods" of water, air, or fire and the many material things derived from the divine first principle. Anaxagoras reached a higher understanding of reality by arguing that the first principle was incorporeal, namely, intellect, but

---

10   M. J. Scheeben, *The Mysteries of Christianity* (St Louis & London: Herder, 1946), 238. Scheeben continues on the same page: "What is supernatural in the angels is what is supernatural in man: the sanctifying grace that makes the rational creature a partaker of the divine nature."
11   Cf. St Thomas Aquinas, *Compendium theologiae* lib. 1, cap. 74; *ST* 1a q. 50, a. 1.
12   St Thomas Aquinas, *De substantiis separatis*, cap. 1.

he too had no place for incorporeal substances below God and above bodily things.

Bodily things are constantly undergoing change, and the senses, by which we know bodily things, are easily deceived; and so the "physicists" (*naturales*, *physikoi*), as Aristotle and Aquinas dub the pre-Socratics, could not see how we can know the truth of reality. Plato's approach, St Thomas suggests, was sounder. He argued that there were natures separate from the flux of materiality, and that in these natures truth abided fixed and unchanging. Our minds, he said, attain the truth by uniting themselves to them. Now there are two kinds of things the human intellect can grasp by separating them from matter: *mathematical things* (numbers, magnitudes, and figures such as triangles) and *universals*, which Plato called the "Forms" or "Ideas" of things (humanness, horseness, and so on). Moreover, among the forms, there was a hierarchy. First came the form of the One-in-Itself and Good-in-Itself, which was the first principle of things. "Under Him, he [Plato, says St Thomas] established diverse orders of participating and participated beings, which he called 'secondary gods.'"[13] In addition to these secondary gods, between God and man, there were also, according to the Platonists, separate intellects, celestial souls, and demons, good or bad. "If all these things were true [St Thomas concludes], then for us [Christians] all these intermediate orders would be called 'angels.'"[14]

Like Aristotle, St Thomas rejects the Platonic doctrine of separate universal ideas. Horseness does not exist in a world of its own. It is found as an idea in the human mind and in the horseflesh of the individual thoroughbreds who run in the Kentucky Derby. St Thomas does not entirely discard Plato's doctrine of the Forms. He makes it his own in the treatises in the *Summa theologiae* on the One God and the angels: the Forms are the ideas of things pre-existing in the mind of the Creator and infused into the minds of His angels.[15]

---

13 Ibid.
14 Ibid.
15 "Since ideas, as posited by Plato, are principles of the knowledge of things and of their generation, an idea, as it exists in the mind of God, has

The more general difficulty with Plato's position is that he postulates, without demonstrating, the existence of the various kinds of separate substances lying between God and man. Aristotle proceeded, says St Thomas, "by a more manifest and surer way, namely, by way of motion."[16] He claims that each of the heavenly bodies is animated by an immaterial soul, and that the complete composite substance is moved by knowledge and desire of a substance that is separate from matter, an altogether immaterial intelligence. For Aristotle, there are as many intelligences as heavenly souls, and as many heavenly souls as motions. "Therefore, according to Aristotle's position, there is only a twofold order of intellectual substances between the Most High God and ourselves, namely, the separate substances, which are the ends of the motions of the heavenly bodies, and the souls of the spheres, which move through appetite and desire."[17]

Angels (or separate substances) are one of the subjects on which St Thomas thought that even Aristotle lost his grip.[18] First, he argues that it is unreasonable to limit, as Aristotle does, the number of immaterial substances to the number of corporeal substances. After all, "higher things do not exist for the sake of the lower; on the contrary, the thing for which something exists is the nobler thing." The heart and the circulation of blood exist to sustain the life of the brain and the animal, not the other way about. Moreover, if you want to know what something is, what it can and cannot

a relation to both. As a principle for making things, the idea can be called an 'exemplar'; in this respect it belongs to practical knowledge. But as a principle of knowledge, the idea is properly called a reason (*ratio*) and can also be part of speculative knowledge. As an exemplar, therefore, it relates to everything made by God at a certain time; whereas as a principle of knowledge it relates to all things known by God, even if they never come to exist in time; and it relates to all things that He knows according to their proper definition (*rationem*), and as known by Him in a speculative manner" (St Thomas Aquinas, *ST* 1a q. 15, a. 3).
16 St Thomas Aquinas, *De substantiis separatis*, cap. 2.
17 Ibid.
18 St Thomas seems never to attribute error to Aristotle when he names him as "the Philosopher," the wise man of all seasons and safe guide to the knowledge of naturally attainable truth, but he does accuse Aristotle *as Aristotle*, the pagan Greek, of numerous errors that he could only have avoided had he been privy to divine revelation.

do, you do not start by studying what exists for the sake of that thing: cardiology is not an adequate introduction to neurology.

> This truth is especially clear in the order of corporeal things, for you cannot discover the magnitude and number of the heavenly bodies from the disposition of the elementary bodies, which are as nothing in comparison to them. Now the immaterial substances surpass corporeal substances much more than the heavenly bodies surpass elementary ones. In view of this, the number, power, and disposition of immaterial substances cannot be adequately grasped from the number of the movements of the heavens.[19]

Secondly, Aristotle and his followers, like Plato before them, were wrong to claim that the angels existed from eternity. "It is contrary to Christian doctrine to say, as the Platonists and Peripatetics claimed, that spiritual substances derive their origin from the supreme Godhead in such a way that they existed from eternity. On the contrary, the Catholic faith asserts that they began to exist after previously not existing."[20] This statement is a particular application of St Thomas's conviction that the world's beginning of existence cannot be proved by natural reason but must be held by faith alone.[21]

Hearing rumors of angels outside the Bible among the poets and philosophers of pagan antiquity should not disturb the Christian mind. "Eliminating a doctrine from revelation on the pretext that you can find rudiments or equivalents of it in non-Biblical religions [says Fr Bonino] derives from an erroneous understanding of the relations between faith and reason, nature and grace, as if grace were bound by definition to contradict nature."[22] Truths supernaturally revealed by God confirm, purify, and elevate, do not contradict or abolish, the religious insights naturally attainable by man.

Despite the mistakes made by the philosophers of antiquity about the number and duration of the separate substances, their

---

19 St Thomas Aquinas, *De substantiis separatis*, cap. 2.
20 St Thomas Aquinas, *De substantiis separatis*, cap. 17. Cf. 1a q. 46, a. 1; SCG lib. 2, cap. 31–38.
21 Cf. *ST* 1a q. 46, a. 2.
22 Bonino, 16.

recognition that the visible universe, even in its highest and most remote parts, is under the influence of spiritual beings, who are less than God but greater than man, is a truth also to be found in Scripture, and, as we shall see, of permanent importance in the theological cosmology of Christendom.

"ON ALMOST EVERY PAGE": THE ANGELS IN SACRED SCRIPTURE

Angels make their appearance in Scripture from Genesis to the Apocalypse, indeed in those opening and closing books of the canon more than in the others. "Almost every page of the sacred text," says St Gregory the Great, "testifies to the existence of angels and archangels."[23] The inspired authors of the Bible give us to understand that the created order is much richer than what we can see with our eyes. Beyond everything visible is a world invisible of simply spiritual persons, who contemplate and worship God in heaven and, in different ways, serve His will on earth. "O ye angels of the Lord, bless the Lord: praise and exalt Him above all forever" (Dan 3:58). Like everything that is not God, the angels are the creatures of God. "He spoke, and they were made; He commanded, and they were created" (Ps 148:5). "For in Him were all things created in heaven and on earth, visible and invisible, whether Thrones or Dominations, or Principalities or Powers. All things were created by Him and for Him" (Col 1:16).

THE NAME AND THE FUNCTION

The word *mal'akh* in the Hebrew Old Testament, like the Greek *angelos*, from which we get our English "angel," means "messenger." It signifies, say St Augustine, not the nature but the function of

---

23   *Homiliae in evangelia*, lib. 2, hom. 34, n. 7; PL 76.1249D. "From the angel of Paradise to the angel of the Apocalypse, who swears there will be no more time, from the angel who appears to Manoah to the one who enlightens Zachariah, from the angels who thrash Heliodorus to the one who guides young Tobias, from the angel who consoles Agar to the one who sets St Peter free, these awe-inspiring, informative, and compassionate brothers of ours make an appearance throughout the whole sacred narrative." Paul Claudel, *Présence et prophétie* (Fribourg: Éditions de la librairie de l'université, 1942), 246.

the angels,[24] for throughout the Bible we find the blessed spirits coming from God to reveal His will to men. Angels press Lot to flee the coming destruction of Sodom (cf. Gen 19:15). It is an angel that stays the hand of Abraham as he raises the knife to slay Isaac; the command to sacrifice his son was a test of his fear of God (cf. Gen 22:11ff). The angel of the Lord appears to Moses in the burning bush in preparation for the revelation of God's name and the commissioning of Moses for leading God's people out of Egypt (cf. Ex 3:2). Later, with the people settled in the promised land, an angel instructs Gideon to deliver Israel out of the hands of Madian (cf. Judg 6:12ff). An angel commands Elijah to rebuke the messengers of the king of Samaria for consulting Beelzebub, the god of Ekron (cf. 4 Kg 1:3).[25]

ST MICHAEL THE ARCHANGEL

The sacred authors of Scripture give personal names to only three angels: Michael, Gabriel, and Raphael. In 741 a Roman synod under Pope Zachary[26] condemned the ascribing to angels of names not derived from the canonical Scriptures.[27] The prophet Daniel calls St Michael "one of the chief princes" (Dan 10:13), a rank that the Apostle Jude renders in Greek as "archangel" (cf. Jude 1:9). Tradition applies the same title to Saints Gabriel and Raphael.

The Hebrew names of the three archangels sum up the mission given them by God. "Michael" means, "Who is like God?"[28] St

---

24 "'Angel' is the name of an office, not a nature. If you want to know the name of the nature, it is 'spirit'; if you want to know the office, it is 'angel.' Because of what he is, he is a spirit; because of what he does, he is an angel. You see the same thing in man: the name of the nature is 'man'; the name of the office is 'soldier'" (St Augustine, *Enarratio in Psalmum 103, sermo* 1, n. 15; PL 37.1349). Lactantius had already said: "We call these 'angels,' which is the name of an office, not a dignity" (*Institutiones*, lib. 1, cap. 7; PL 6.150B). St Augustine's clarification becomes a commonplace of the tradition (cf. St Gregory the Great, *Homiliae in evangelia*, lib. 2, Homilia 34; PL 76.1250C; Hugh of St Victor, *Quaestiones et decisiones in epistolas D. Pauli, In epistolam ad Hebraeos*, q. 16; PL 175.613B).

25 The angels are also called "sons of God" (cf. Job 1:6; 2:1).

26 Cf. J. D. Mansi, *Sacrorum conciliorum nova et amplissima collectio*, t. 12 (Florence: Zatta, 1766), 379–80.

27 Cf. Mansi, 384.

28 Cf. St Gregory the Great, *Homilia* 34, n. 9; PL 76.1251B.

Michael is the guardian of the Jewish people, whom the one true God specially chose to bear witness to Him as the Creator of all things and Lord of history. The angel Gabriel says to Daniel, when he asks God to allow the Jews to return to Jerusalem: "The prince of the kingdom of the Persians resisted me ... and, behold Michael, one of the chief princes, came to help me ... and none is my helper in all these things but Michael your prince" (Dan 10:13, 21).[29] Daniel also prophesies the part played by St Michael, protector of Israel both old and new, in the last scene of the drama of human history: "At that time shall Michael rise up, the great prince, who standeth for the children of thy people" (Dan 12:1). In the revelation given him by God through an angel (cf. Apoc 1:1), St John speaks in more detail of St Michael's final victory over the devil, which is a recapitulation of their first conflict, when Lucifer and his angels fell into eternal damnation:

> And there was a great battle in heaven. Michael and his angels fought with the dragon, and the dragon fought and his angels, and they prevailed not; neither was their place found anymore in heaven. And that great dragon was cast out, that old serpent, who is called

---

29   If "prince" means the holy guardian angel of a nation, how can one holy angel "resist" another? The conflict would seem to make sense only if the angel of the Persians were a demon. But St Gregory suggests that the prince of the Persians was in fact the nation's holy guardian angel. *In themselves*, the guardian angels of the nations are united in obedience to God's will; it is in the differences of the nations they serve that conflict arises. The angels execute God's judgments in relation to nations that differ in morality and merit as well as culture. Now the angels of nations in conflict have incomplete knowledge of the merits of one nation and the demerits of the other. Therefore, as best he can, the angel of the Persians serves Divine Providence by protecting the people and guiding their rulers, while St Michael does the same for the Jews. "The angels cannot know what the plan of Divine Wisdom is in regard to these matters, unless God reveal it to them: and so they need to consult Divine wisdom about them. Hence, insofar as they consult God's will about the contrary and opposing merits [of those they guard], they are said to resist each other: not that their wills are in opposition, since they all agree that God's decree should be fulfilled, but because the things about which they consult are in opposition" (St Thomas, ST 1a q. 113, a. 8). The holy angels, in the eternal peace of heaven, are not in conflict with each other; it is the men and nations they serve who start fights and wage war.

the devil and Satan, who seduceth the whole world; and he was cast unto the earth, and his angels were thrown down with him. (Apoc 12:7–9)

St Michael, prince of the heavenly host, is the great soldier, the war hero, among the angels of God.

From the world's first days to its last, St Michael is the punisher of the devil's arrogance; in Dante's words, he takes "vengeance on the proud adultery."[30] He wages war against Satan, so·that "he who in his pride had elevated himself to the likeness of God should in his confounding learn that no one can rise up by pride to the likeness of God."[31] St Michael's name — "Who is like God?" — teaches presumptuous creatures that God is He Who Is, and that they, lofty Seraphim like lowly snails, are mere nothings.

ST GABRIEL THE ARCHANGEL

St Gabriel explains the meaning of a vision to the prophet Daniel: "I will show thee what things are to come to pass in the end of the malediction, for this time hath its end" (Dan 8:19). It is he who tells Zechariah that his barren wife will at last give birth, and that their son, John, filled with the Holy Spirit, will prepare the way for the Lord (cf. Lk 1:13ff). Six months later, St Gabriel is "sent from God" on the greatest angelic mission of all, when he arrives in bodily form in Nazareth to bring the glad tidings of the Incarnation of the Son of God to Mary, the Virgin betrothed to Joseph of the house of David (cf. Lk 1:26f).[32] In Paradise, says Dante, this "angel of joyous gaze" looks "into the eyes of our sweet Queen — / so deeply in love, he seems to be ablaze."[33] His name

---

30 *Inferno* 7, 12; Sayers, 110. "Adultery" (*strupo*) is used here, according to Sayers, "in the Biblical sense of unfaithfulness to God — as in 'whoring after strange gods'" (Sayers, 115).
31 Cf. St Gregory the Great, *Homilia* 34, n. 9; PL 76.1251B.
32 There are three reasons why at the Annunciation the angel should have appeared as the possessor of a body: first, it is fitting that an invisible creature should come in visible form to announce the Incarnation of the invisible God; secondly, the Mother of God conceived the Word not only in her mind but also in her bodily womb; and, thirdly, we human beings more readily grasp what we see with our eyes than what we experience in our imagination (cf. St Thomas, *ST* 3a q. 30, a. 3).
33 *Paradiso* 32, 104–5; Esolen, 347.

means "strength of God," because he announces the coming of the Lord, "strong and mighty," in the humility of human flesh.[34]

ST RAPHAEL THE ARCHANGEL

Raphael means "medicine of God."[35] It is an appropriate name, because he is the one who tells Tobias to cure the blindness of his father, the faithful Jew, Tobias Senior, by anointing his eyes with the gall of a fish (cf. Tob 11:13ff). St Raphael, in Dante's words, is he "by whom old Tobit found amending."[36] Once he has accomplished the mission entrusted to him by God, Raphael reveals his identity: "The Lord hath sent me to heal thee, and to deliver Sara, thy son's wife, from the devil. For I am the angel Raphael, one of the seven who stand before the Lord" (Tob 12:14f).

THE HOST OF HEAVEN

The created spirits form an army, the "host of Heaven" (cf. 3 Kg 22:19), and so, like every army, have a command structure with higher and lower ranks. Highest of all the ranks, by the clarity of their vision and the ardor of their love, are the *Seraphim*, the six-winged flying furnaces, who sing "Holy, Holy, Holy" to the Lord God of Hosts and burn away the sins of the prophet Isaiah with a coal (cf. Is 6:1ff). Next in glory are the *Cherubim*,[37] upon whom God sits as on a throne (cf. 1 Sam 4:4; Ps 79:1, 98:1). He rides upon them (cf. Ps 17:10) as if they were the platform of His chariot; when they carry Him, their four wings clap with the sound of thunder (cf. Ezek 10:20). When God sends Adam out of the Garden of Eden, "to till the ground from which he was taken," He stations the Cherubim "to guard the way to the tree of life" (cf. Gen 3:23f). Large images of the Cherubim stand facing each other on the Ark of the Covenant, their wings outspread over the Mercy-Seat, and from between them the Lord speaks to Israel (cf. Ex 25:22). In his epistles St Paul supplies the names

---

34 Cf. St Gregory the Great, *Homilia* 34, n. 9; PL 76.1251B.
35 Cf. St Gregory the Great, *Homilia* 34, n. 9; PL 76.1251C.
36 *Paradiso* 4, 48; Sayers-Reynolds, 82.
37 Cf. R. G. Ilboa, "Cherubim: An Inquiry into an Enigma," *Biblische Notizen* 82 (1996), 59–75.

of five other groupings: *Virtues, Powers, Principalities, Dominations,* and *Thrones* (cf. Eph 1:21; Col 1:16). These, together with the *Archangels*[38] and *Angels* revealed to the patriarchs, prophets, and apostles, make up the nine orders of the angels.

GOOD ANGELS AND BAD

We learn from Sacred Scripture that there are bad angels as well as good. The good are called "holy angels" (cf. Mk 8:38). They do good things for human beings, as Raphael did, healing and guiding them (cf. Tob 3:25; 5). Angels who behold the face of the Father in Heaven guard the little ones on earth (cf. Mt 18:10). God has given His angels charge over men, to guard them (cf. Ps 90:11). The bad angels are the demons, who tempt and attack human beings. The devil is the "adversary" of man, and "as a roaring lion goeth about, seeking whom he may devour" (1 Pt 5:8). According to the inspired authors of Sacred Scripture, the devil and his demons are angels, who were created good and true by God, but fell into being evil and untruthful by their own free action.

> The angels...did not keep their own position, but left their proper dwelling, [and] have been kept by Him in eternal chains in the nether gloom until the judgment of the great day. (Jude 6)

> God did not spare the angels when they sinned, but cast them into hell, and committed them to pits of nether gloom to be kept until the judgment. (2 Peter 2:4)

> [The devil] stood not in the truth. (Jn 8:44)[39]

"The gods of the Gentiles are devils" (Ps 95:5), says David in the older translation of that verse, for only devils would induce men to do what Israel's neighbors and the apostate Israelites did, namely, sacrifice their own children as holocausts (cf. Ps 105:37). In the book of Job (cf. Job 1:6ff), Satan makes his first appearance under that name: he is a fallen creature, and does his tempting only by divine permission, and never without the tempted man

---

38 The prophet Daniel calls Michael "one of the chief princes" (Dan 10:13).
39 The demonology of the tradition is discussed below in ch. 4, 113ff.

being strengthened by God's grace to withstand him. St Thomas Aquinas points out that in Scripture the names of seven of the angelic orders, since they signify the obedient service of God, are not attributed to the fallen angels. But there are demonic Principalities and Powers, because they are "powerful and great, and so have a great army, against which we have to fight."[40]

MINISTERING SPIRITS

The angels play leading roles in the drama of salvation, yet never perform center-stage. They are servants of the servants of God. "Are they not all ministering spirits, sent to minister for them who shall receive the inheritance of salvation?" (Heb 1:14).[41] The holy angels are always *surprising*. They appear to the saints without warning or invitation, for the time and the purpose of their earthly mission depend solely upon the infinite wisdom and incomprehensible will of God. That is why "some have entertained angels unawares" (Heb 13:2).

In the history of the patriarchs in Genesis, and again in Exodus, encounters with angels are "theophanies," manifestations of God. The most important example is the arrival of three angels in human form at Abraham's tent by the oaks of Mamre (cf. Gen 18:1ff). The narrative's strange alternation in subject between God and His angels is a sign that, though the angels differ from their Creator in essence and existence, they of all creatures are closest to Him, and so, when the message they bring from God is welcomed and heeded, they make the men they address partake of their own intimacy with God. Some of the Fathers see these angelic visitations as a type and promise of the Incarnation, a preparatory revelation of the Word.[42] The one who fights with Jacob (cf. Gen 32:22–36) is described as "a man," but he inspires fear and has immense strength. "He is 'the angel of the Lord' [says Romano

---

40   St Thomas, *Super epistolam Beati Pauli ad Ephesios lectura*, cap. 6, lect. 3.
41   David places "angels" (messengers) in parallelism with "minister" (cf. Ps 103:4).
42   Cf. St Justin Martyr, "Christ is Lord, God, the Son of God. He first appeared in power as a man and an angel, and in a glory of fire in the Bush" (*Dialogus cum Tryphone* cap. 128; PG 6.773–76).

Guardini] with a nature beyond human comprehension, a finite creature yet, as becomes clear in v. 30, somehow God Himself."[43]

The masters of sacred doctrine regard the visit of three angels to Abraham as a foreshadowing of the revelation of the Trinity of Persons in God. "The Arians claimed [says St Thomas] that in various visions in the Old Testament the Son appears, but not the Father. This is shown to be false by the fact that three men appeared to Abraham as a symbol of the Trinity."[44] As St Augustine says, *Abraham tres vidit et unum adoravit*, "Abraham beheld the Three, but worshipped the One."[45]

The blessed spirits appear to the patriarchs in bodily form and interest themselves in the material complexities of human life. In their dealings with men, the citizens of the heavenly Jerusalem are always down-to-earth. The holy angels, in the sublimity of their spirituality and their grounding in the truth, have no interest in the madness of angelism.

THE ANGELS AND THE WORSHIP OF GOD

Wherever Israel, old or new, worships the true God, the angels are in attendance: "I will sing praise to thee in the sight of the angels" (Ps 138:1). "Bless the Lord, all ye His angels," says David (cf. Ps 102:20), and Daniel, too: "O ye angels of the Lord, bless ye the Lord" (3:58). Isaiah hears the Seraphim singing the threefold *Sanctus* to the Lord: "Holy, holy, holy Lord God of Hosts" (cf. Is 6:3). In the Apocalypse of St John, the heavenly city resounds with the melody of the same canticle, to which the angels and saints add praise of the slain and glorious Lamb: "Then I looked, and I heard around the throne and the living creatures and the elders the voice of many angels, numbering myriads of myriads and thousands of thousands, saying with a loud voice, 'Worthy is the Lamb who was slain, to receive power and wealth and wisdom and might and honor and glory and blessing'" (Apoc 5:11–12).

43 Romano Guardini, *Der Engel*, 33.
44 *Super decretales*, n. 1.
45 Cf. St Augustine, *Contra Maximinum haereticum* cap 16, n. 7; PL 42.809; Blessed Denys the Carthusian, *Enarratio in cap. 18 Gen.* a. 57; DCOO 1.256D–256A.

THE LORD JESUS: THE HEAD OF THE ANGELS

The New Testament shows us, in the *Catechism's* words, that the Lord Jesus is "the center of the angelic world ... From the Incarnation to the Ascension, the life of the Word made flesh is surrounded by the adoration and service of the angels."[46] The blessed spirits are the angels of the Son of Man (cf. Mt. 13:41); they belong to Him, and serve Him, in His humanity as well as in His divinity. According to St Paul, they were created by, in, and for Christ (cf. Col 1:16). He is the Head of the angels, as He is the Head of men: "You are filled in him who is the Head of all principality and power" (Col. 2:10). His Mystical Body counts angels as well as men among its members. As their Head, our Lord is above the angels and has an influence over them.[47] In His divine nature, He is infinitely above them; He is their Creator. As the Apostle says, to which of the angels does God the Father say, "Thou art my Son, today [that is, in the day of eternity] have I begotten thee" (cf. Heb 1:5)? In His human nature, too, Christ is above all the angels. God the Father has set Him "on His right hand in the heavenly places, above all Principality and Power and Virtue and Dominion and every name that is named not only in this world, but also in that which is to come. And He hath subjected all things under his feet" (Eph 1:20ff).[48]

How does Christ the Head, as man, *influence* the angels? Head and members should share a common nature, but Christ, the Son of God, assumed not the purely spiritual nature of the angels, but the composite nature of man, a material body animated by a spiritual and rational soul. Now, the influence of the Word made flesh on men is felt chiefly in their souls, the part of their nature that connects them with the angels. Therefore, because of that bond in spirit, the incarnate Son can also be said to be of influence on the angels.[49] The human nature of Christ, united hypostatically to the divine nature, which is spiritual, "can cause

---

46 CCC 331 and 333.
47 Cf. *ST* 3a q. 8, a. 4.
48 Cf. *ST* 3a q. 8, a. 4.
49 Cf. *ST* 3a q. 8, a. 4, ad 1.

something not only in the spirits of men, but in the spirits of angels."[50] When he discusses our Lord's power as judge, St Thomas explains in more detail how this causality works. Because of the closeness of the assumed human nature to God, the soul of Christ is "more filled with the truth of the Word of God than any of the angels is, and so, as Denys says, he sheds his light even on the angels."[51] The soul of Christ, says Fr Bonino, "knows far better than the highest of the angels God's most intimate designs, and is in a position to reveal them to them."[52] The grace of Christ as Head of men is *redemptive*, a grace that both heals the sons of Adam and elevates them to supernatural life as the adopted sons of God. By contrast, the angels are neither sons of Adam nor creatures capable of redemption; they enjoy heavenly glory because they cooperated with, and did not resist, the grace given them in their first state; the grace of the angels was elevating but not redemptive. Our Lord did not merit the essential glory of the angels on the Cross, nor did He pray for them, as He did for men. However, Christ as man influences the angels through the accidental rewards they enjoy in heaven, namely, their joy in His saving of sinful men: "So, I say to you, there shall be joy before the angels of God upon one sinner doing penance" (Lk 15:10).

THE WORD MADE FLESH AND THE BODILESS POWERS

The first duty of the angels who serve the Word made flesh is to bear witness to His divinity. He applies to himself Jacob's vision of the angels ascending and descending on a ladder connecting earth with heaven (cf. Gen 28:12; Jn 1:51). According to St John Chrysostom and St Thomas, by these words "our Lord wishes to prove that he is the true Son of God and God, for the proper task of angels is to minister and be subject.... 'So, when you see angels ministering to me, you will be certain that I am the true Son of God.'"[53] Jesus, the eternal Son of God, is "the

50 *ST* 3a q. 8, a. 4, ad 3.
51 Cf. *ST* 3a q. 59, a. 6.
52 Bonino, 231.
53 St Thomas Aquinas, *Super Ioannem* cap. 1, lect. 16.

brightness of [the Father's] glory and the figure of His substance," and therefore infinitely superior to the angels (cf. Heb 1:3f). To no angel did God ever say, "Thou art my Son, today [in the day of the divine eternity] have I begotten thee" (Heb 1:5). Therefore, "let all the angels of God adore him" (Heb 1:6).

The angels are also the heavenly witnesses to the reality of the human nature assumed by God the Son into the unity of person, and to all that He suffered or accomplished in human nature for the salvation of mankind. They are therefore the sworn foes of every diabolical heresy—from Gnosticism to Modernism—that runs in flight from the flesh of the divine Savior. In all the mysteries of our Lord's life on earth, the holy angels keep Him company and do Him service, just as the wicked angels taunt and attack Him. The angels of Christ have as their watchword *caro salutis est cardo*, "the flesh is the hinge of salvation."[54] By speaking and acting from their great height, the blessed spirits point to the depths to which the eternal Son descends when, without ceasing to be God, He becomes man. The mission of the good created spirits, like that of the uncreated Holy Spirit, is always to lead men to the Son in His humanity, and only in that way to reach Him in His divinity with the Father and the Holy Spirit. The angels bear witness to God the Son, and worship Him, in His self-emptying, in the humility of the form of a servant (cf. Phil. 2:7–8). This mission of the angels is evident in the iconography of the Annunciation. Fra Angelico's archangel Gabriel *kneels* before Mary, as he tells her she is to conceive and give human birth to the "Son of the Most High" (cf. Lk 1:26). At Bethlehem, "a multitude of the heavenly army" sing *Gloria in excelsis Deo* to acclaim the human and temporal birth of the Son of God in the poverty of a stable (cf. Lk 2:13f). An angel reveals to St Joseph in a dream that he must take care of the Blessed Virgin and the Child, conceived by the Holy Spirit, whom she bears within her womb (cf. Mt 1:20). Later the angel tells Joseph to take the newborn Savior, with His Virgin Mother, into the safety of Egypt

---

54   Tertullian, *De resurrectione carnis* cap. 8; PL 2.806A.

(cf. Mt 2:13), and to return after Herod's death (cf. v. 19f). The God-Man walks with feet of flesh upon this earth with all its dangers. To this truth, too, the ministering spirits testify.

In the wilderness, Jesus does not receive the attentions of the angels until He has inflicted defeat upon the devil (cf. Mt. 4:11). He does not yield to Satan's suggestion that He deploy the angels for a spectacular display of His powers (cf. Mt 4:6; Ps 90:11). On Mount Olivet, only when Jesus has endured sorrow unto death, and surrendered His human will to the Father, does the angel come to console Him (cf. Lk 22:39ff). Even so He then goes back to the fray, His sweat falling as thick drops of blood upon the ground (cf. Lk 22:44). He could, but does not, ask the Father to dispatch more than twelve legions of angels to rescue Him (cf. Mt 26:53). No man takes His life away; He lays it down of Himself (cf. Jn 10:18). With the perfect freedom of His human will, in obedience to the Father's saving plan, and out of love for us men in our infirmity, the Son abandons all protection in His Passion. The angels must stand back, and wait patiently for Easter Sunday, though on Good Friday, if Giotto is right, they weep tears of immaterial sorrow.[55]

Only after death's Conqueror has come up from Hades in His human soul and risen gloriously from the tomb in His human body do the angels appear again on earth, this time in the form of young men with shining faces and clothes of dazzling white (cf. Mt 28:2–7; Mk 16:5; Lk 24:4; Jn 20:12). Blessed spirits though they are, these first evangelists of Easter tolerate no turning of body into spirit: they certify the Savior's Resurrection in the flesh. One of them rolls the stone away from the entrance to the Tomb — the work of a moment for an angel — so that its emptiness may be visible to all: "He is not here, for he is risen [in the very body that once lay here], as he said. Come, and see the place where the Lord was laid" (cf. Mt 28:6). St Mary Magdalene sees two angels in the empty tomb in the very place where our Lord's body had been placed, one at the head and

55 Cf. the fresco of the *Lamentation* in the Scrovegni chapel in Padua.

one at the feet (cf. Jn 20:12). The heavenly messengers are pure spirits, but the risen Lord is not: He is alive in His complete humanity, in soul and body, in flesh and blood, from head to toe, in every pore and bone. Forty days later, as the disciples stare astonished at Jesus ascending into heaven in His glorified human body, the angels — appearing in the form of two men in white garments — stand beside them on earth, reminding them that the same Jesus will come down again to earth in the same way, in the same glorified humanity, in which they have seen Him go up into heaven (cf. Acts 1:11).

By taking upon himself human flesh and blood and the seed of Abraham rather than a grand angelic nature (cf. Heb 2:16), the Son makes himself a little less than the angels (cf. Heb 2:7), just as in the humiliation of His Passion He makes himself like a worm and not a man (cf. Ps 21:6). In the glorious exaltation of His Resurrection and Ascension, His superiority is finally and eternally revealed: His humanity is elevated high "above all Principality and Power and Virtue and Domination" (cf. Eph 1:21). At His Second Coming, our Lord will not again take up the path of infirmity and obscurity; He will arrive in splendor, in the glory of His Father and with an open display of His lordship of the angels (cf. Mt 16:27). They will serve Him as judge by separating the wicked from the just (cf. Mt 13:49) and gathering the elect "from the four winds, from the farthest parts of the heavens to the utmost bounds of them" (Mt 24:31). Meanwhile, in the time of the Church's pilgrimage, the holy angels serve Christ in the members of His Mystical Body (cf. Heb 1:14). The angel of the Lord opens the prison door for the apostles to escape (cf. Acts 5:19), rescues St Peter from the hands of Herod (cf. Acts 12:7–11), and saves St Paul from death at sea, so that he can stand and bear witness to Christ before Caesar (cf. Acts 27:23).

In the Apocalypse, Heaven is revealed as the place where the numberless hosts of the angels worship God and the Lamb, glorious and ever slain (cf. Apoc 5:11–12). The Empyrean is not empty till the just of the Old Testament arrive there after our Lord has delivered them from the Limbo of the Fathers in His descent into hell. When they reach the summit of the heavenly Zion, the patriarchs and prophets join a commonwealth of already blessed creatures, thousands upon thousands of angels "in festal gathering," enjoying the bliss of beholding the Holy Trinity (cf. Heb 12:22f).

"THE INTELLIGENT HIERARCHIES OF HEAVEN": THE ANGELOLOGY OF THE FATHERS

All the Fathers, from the earliest years of the post-apostolic age onwards, testify to the existence of the angels. In exhorting the Corinthian Christians to have confidence in God, and to show Him obedience, St Clement of Rome invites them to consider the example of the angels, who "stand by and minister unto His will."[56]

In the last book of *The City of God*, when speaking of the beatific vision, St Augustine says that the holy angels are "*our* angels, because we, having been delivered from the power of darkness and received the pledge of the Spirit, have been translated into the Kingdom of Christ, and have already begun to be united to those angels with whom we shall share that holy and most sweet City of God of which we have now written so much."[57] As for the moment of their creation, his final opinion is that they were created at the same time as the visible universe. When the first sentence of the Bible says, "God made heaven and earth," by "heaven" is meant "not the corporeal heaven, but the incorporeal heaven, which is placed above all bodies, not by level of location, but by sublimity of nature."[58] The six days of creation are not a stretch of time, but a series of illuminations by which the minds of the angels have knowledge of creatures. When the sacred author speaks of "morning," he is referring to the knowledge by which the angels know things in God, that is, in the Word in whom God says, "Let it be done," and it is done.[59] The "evening" is the knowledge the angels have of things in themselves as distinct from

56 *Epistola ad Corinthios* cap. 34; *The Apostolic Fathers: Revised Texts with Short Introductions and English Translations*, by J. B. Lightfoot (London: Macmillan, 1907), 71.
57 *De civitate Dei* lib. 22, cap. 29, n. 1; PL 41.797.
58 *De Genesi ad litteram* lib. 1, cap. 17, n. 32; PL34.258.
59 *De Genesi ad litteram* lib. 4, cap. 26, n. 43; PL 34.314.

God.[60] Moreover, he says that everything in the universe, every bodily creature, "has an angelic power placed over it."[61]

Greatest of all the Patristic angelologists is the mystic and doctor of the Greek Church who hides himself behind the name of the Areopagite, St Paul's Athenian convert (cf. Acts 17:34). We should not insult him with the prefix "Pseudo," but should honor him, as St Thomas does, with the title "Blessed."[62] In the *Celestial Hierarchy* he supplies the tradition, on the basis of Scripture, with the ordering of the angelic world. He describes the light that flows from the Father of lights into the angels closest to Him, from them into the lower levels, and thence upon the mind of man. The earthly hierarchy of the Church, which is an image of the "intellectual hierarchies of heaven,"[63] is the God-founded instrument of illumination, of the splendor of truth, in this world.[64]

In Denys's understanding, a hierarchy is not a system of domination, but "a sacred order" of divinization, enabling intellectual creatures "to be as much like God as possible, and to be united with Him."[65] The "holy ranks of heavenly beings" are superior to us in what they have received from their Creator. Their intellects more closely resemble the mind of God and are more perfectly illuminated by Him. Their "whole life is intellectual," and from

---

60 *De Genesi ad litteram* lib. 4, 30, n. 47; PL 34.316. "[The angels] were made partakers of the eternal light that is the unchangeable Wisdom of God Himself, through whom all things were made, and whom we call the only-begotten Son of God. They were illuminated by the Light that created them, and were called 'day' by sharing in that unchangeable Light and Day which is the Word of God, through whom they themselves and everything else were made" (*De civitate Dei* lib. 11, cap. 9, PL 41.325).
61 *Liber 83 quaestionum* q. 79; PL 40.90. See 90ff. below.
62 E.g. SCG lib 2, cap. 68, n. 2.
63 *De caelesti hierarchia* cap. 1, n. 2; PG 3.120A.
64 "He made our own hierarchy a concelebrant of those divine hierarchies by making it, as far as is possible, like their divine priesthood" (*De caelesti hierarchia* cap. 1, n. 3; PG 3.136B). "Denys describes a universe of beauty and intelligible harmony on its way to divinization. The Blessed Trinity, in Its inexhaustible generosity, communicates something of Its perfection to creatures, but It does so progressively, in a 'hierarchical' order, which concerns, first, the angels (the heavenly hierarchies) and then men (the ecclesiastical hierarchy)." Bonino, 60.
65 *De caelesti hierarchia* cap. 3, n. 2; PG 3.165A.

their enlightenment by God we receive "revelations that are beyond us."[66] The lowest rank of the heavenly hierarchy bears the simple name "angel" ("messenger"), but all the blessed spirits above them also deserve the name, for "they too make known the enlightenment proceeding from the Deity."[67]

CONCELEBRATING WITH THE SERAPHIM: THE ANGELS IN THE SACRED LITURGY

In the Church's liturgy, in its Eastern and traditional Western forms, the angels are everywhere. In the *Confiteor* of the *usus antiquior* of the Roman Mass we confess to Blessed Michael the Archangel as we do to almighty God, Blessed Mary Ever-Virgin, and all the angels and saints. Denys the Carthusian says that in the ninefold *Kyrie* we ask the Three-Personed God, by His mercy, to take us up into the nine orders of the angels.[68] In the *Gloria* we echo the angels' song above Bethlehem. The censing of the altar at the Offertory of a Sung or Solemn Mass receives a blessing from God through the intercession of St Michael "standing on the right hand of the altar of incense." In the Preface we join with the Angels, Dominations, Powers, Virtues, and Seraphim in social exultation and concelebrant praise of the thrice-holy God. The priest in the Roman Canon prays for the Sacrifice to be "borne by the hands of [God's] holy angel to [His] altar on high."[69] These are words of deep mystery. St Thomas says they do not signify a local movement of the sacred species, nor of the true Body of Christ really present beneath them. They are best understood of Christ's *Mystical* Body:

---

66 *De caelesti hierarchia* cap. 4, n. 2; PG 3.180B.
67 *De caelesti hierarchia* cap. 5; .PG 3.196D.
68 Cf. Blessed Denys, *Expositio missae*, art. 9; DCOO 35.340BC.
69 Cf. the Secret of the Feast of the Dedication of St Michael on September 29 in the *Missale romanum* (1962): "We offer thee the Sacrifice of praise, O Lord, and humble beseech thee that, through the prayers of thy holy angels, who plead for us, thou wouldst graciously receive it, and grant that it may avail us unto salvation." In the Liturgy of St Mark in the Coptic rite, the priest prays: "Accept, O God, by your ministering archangels, at your holy, heavenly, and reasonable altar in the spacious heavens, the thank-offerings of those who offer sacrifice and oblation." See Odilo Heiming OSB, "Der Engel in der Liturgie," in *Die Engel in der Welt von heute*, ed. Theodor Bogler, OSB (Maria Laach: Ars Liturgica, 1957), 43–49.

the priest asks that the angel may take up to heaven his and his people's prayers on earth, all the intentions by which they unite themselves to the Eternal High Priest and Victim in His self-offering. The priest prays for a participation in the "altar on high" (*sublime altare*), which is either, says St Thomas, the Church Triumphant, into which we ask to be taken, or God Himself, the coequal Trinity, in whose life we pray for participation. It may be, too, that the angel, using the term by analogy, is Christ himself, "the Angel of the Great Counsel" (cf. Is 9:6), "who joins his Mystical Body to the Father and the Church Triumphant."[70] One of Tradition's explanations of the name *Missa* is that in the Eucharistic Sacrifice we have a Victim, Christ, sent (*missa*) to us by God, and so, when the deacon sings, *Ite missa est*, he means that the divine Victim has now been sent to God through the angel and accepted by God.[71]

The calendar of the 1962 edition of the *Missale romanum* contains four feasts dedicated to the angels: the feast of St Gabriel on the eve of the Annunciation, March 24; of the Dedication of St Michael on September 29, which not only commemorates the dedication of a church to St Michael,[72] but also celebrates all the "angels who stand before God's face to minister to [Him] in Heaven";[73] of the Holy Guardian Angels on October 2; and of St Raphael, the archangel of healing, on October 24.

Before death, the Latin Church's priests invite the departing soul to go forth in the name of the holy angels and pray that Satan and his minions "may tremble with fear and flee into the monstrous chaos of unending night." After death, when the body is carried off for interment, the Church sings: *In paradisum deducant te angeli*, "May the angels lead thee into Paradise.... May a choir of angels welcome thee, and with Lazarus, once poor, mayest thou

---

70 Cf. *ST* 3a q. 83, a. 4, ad 9.
71 Cf. ibid.
72 It is not certain which church of St Michael has its feast of dedication on September 29. Before 1962 the *Missale romanum* had a feast of St Michael on May 8, commemorating the dedication of the church of St Michael on Monte Gargano in southern Italy. The holy archangel is believed to have appeared in this place in the late fifth century, and to have asked for a church to be built.
73 From the collect of Michaelmas Day.

have eternal rest," words echoed by Shakespeare when he makes Horatio say over the dead body of Hamlet, "Good night, sweet prince; and flights of angels sing thee to thy rest."[74]

Abbot Vonier points to the boldness with which in the traditional Roman Ritual the Church asks for angelic intervention whenever she blesses things or human persons:

> If the Church blesses a bridge over a river, she confidently expects that an angel will be deputed to the keeping of that bridge. The Church prays God to join His angel to the chariot on which her blessing has been bestowed. The angels are called down to the house of the sick, into the home of the newly wed, into the rooms where Christ's little ones are being taught their faith and their letters. There seems to be no end to these angelic possibilities in the sense of the Catholic Church. Everywhere the evil spirits are driven away, and the good spirits are made to take their place.[75]

In the Byzantine Liturgy of St John Chrysostom, from beginning to end, the Church unites herself to the celestial hierarchy of the angels in their worship of God. In the Prayer of the Entrance, the priest prays the Lord our God to grant that, "with our entrance, holy angels may enter, concelebrating with us, and with us glorifying your goodness."[76] In the Prayer of the Trisagion, God, the Holy One, "at rest in the holy place," who brought all things into being and created man in His image, is said to be "hymned by the Seraphim with the thrice-holy song, glorified by the Cherubim, and worshipped by every heavenly power."[77] At the Great Entrance, as the faithful venerate the holy gifts in anticipation of what they will later become by Transubstantiation, the choir sings, in "a slow and solemn melody," the Cherubic Hymn, and the people bow low: "We, who in a mystery represent the Cherubim and sing the thrice-holy hymn to the life-giving Trinity, let us

---

74 *Hamlet* act 5, scene 2, lines 308–9; William Shakespeare, *Complete Works*, ed. Jonathan Bate & Eric Rasmusen (London: Macmillan, 2007), 1998.
75 Vonier, *Teaching*, 252.
76 *Divine Liturgy*, 11.
77 Ibid., 12.

now lay aside every care of this life. For we are about to receive the King of all, invisibly escorted by the angelic hosts."[78] In the prayer that follows, the priest proclaims that "to serve [God] is great and awesome even for the heavenly powers,"[79] and continues: "For you alone, Lord our God, are ruler over all things in heaven and on earth, mounted on the throne of the Cherubim, Lord of the Seraphim and King of Israel, the only Holy One, resting in the holy place."[80] In the Liturgy of St James, we are told that, when Christ our God becomes present "to be sacrificed and given for food to the faithful," He is "preceded by the choirs of the angels, with every Domination and Power, the many-eyed Cherubim, and the six-winged Seraphim, that cover their faces, and vociferate the hymn, Alleluia, Alleluia, Alleluia."[81]

In the Byzantine equivalent of the Latin Preface, the priest thanks God "for this liturgy which [He has] been pleased to accept from our hands, though there stand around [Him] thousands of archangels and tens of thousands, the Cherubim and the Seraphim, six-winged and many-eyed, soaring aloft upon their wings, singing, crying, shouting the triumphal hymn, and saying: 'Holy, holy, holy.'"[82] "With these blessed powers," the celebrant proceeds to the Consecration, praising the Father, with the Son and the Holy Spirit, as "holy . . . and all-holy, and magnificent in [His] glory."[83] But, after the Epiclesis, in the great hymn *Axion estin*, the Church reminds us that even the highest of the angels are immeasurably inferior in glory to the Ever-Virgin Mother of Him whose true Body and Precious Blood now lie upon the altar under the appearances of

---

78   Ibid., 22. There are two feasts of St Michael in the Byzantine calendar: on September 6 the Miracle of St Michael at Chonai in southwest Asia Minor, and on November 8 the Synaxis of St Michael the Archangel and All Angels. The Copts not only commemorate St Michael on June 19 but observe the twelfth of each month of the year as a day of special devotion to the angels.
79   Ibid.
80   Ibid., 23.
81   *The Liturgies of Saints Mark, James, Clement, Chrysostom, and Basil, and the Church of Malabar*, translated, with introduction and appendices, by the Rev. J. M. Neale DD and the Rev. R. F. Littledale LL.D, second edition (London: Hayes, 1869), 38f.
82   *Divine Liturgy*, 31.
83   Ibid., 32.

bread and wine: "It is truly right to call you blessed, who gave birth to God, ever blessed and most pure, and Mother of our God. Greater in honor than the Cherubim and beyond compare more glorious than the Seraphim, without corruption you gave birth to God; truly the Mother of God, we magnify you."[84] At the end of the Liturgy, the priest gives the blessing through the intercession of the Mother of God and all the saints and "the protection of the honored, bodiless powers of Heaven."[85] The faithful leave the church, with the sacramental presence within them of the King of glory, and sheltered beneath the wings of His holy angels.

Remembering the presence and ministry of the angels in the Sacred Liturgy ought to dispose us to "active participation" in the Mass, that full engagement of mind and heart by which we unite ourselves to the priest on earth as he offers, and still more to Christ, our Head and Eternal High Priest, as through the earthly priest He renews for us His self-offering to the Father in adoration and thanksgiving, in propitiation and supplication.[86] The liturgy of the Church, especially the divine liturgy of the Sacrifice of the Mass, is a concelebration with the angels.[87] Every congregation at Holy Mass, be it large or small, is surrounded by the blessed spirits who worship the Lamb both in the heights of the Empyrean and on the altars of the Church on earth. As Eric Peterson argues in his classic work *The Angels and the Liturgy*, "all acts of worship ... have to be seen ... as a participation by the angels in earthly worship, or, conversely, the worship of the Church upon earth has to be seen as a participation in that worship which is offered to God in heaven by the angels."[88] The divine liturgy of

84 Ibid., 35.
85 Ibid., 51.
86 Cf. Pope Pius XII's Encyclical Letter *Mediator Dei* (November 20, 1947); AAS 39 (1947), 521–95.
87 "The heavens, and the Virtues of the heavens, and the blessed Seraphim concelebrate in social exultation" (Common Preface in the *Missale romanum* of 1962 and earlier editions).
88 *The Angels and the Liturgy* (London: Darton, Longman & Todd, 1964), xi. "We believe that the angelic spirits are especially present when we enter church and give ear to the sacred lessons, or work hard at the Psalms, or apply ourselves to prayer, or celebrate the solemnities of Mass" (St Bede the Venerable, *Homilia 4, infra octavas Paschae*; PL 94.151C).

the Mass, says Abbot Gérard Calvet of Le Barroux, fulfils Jacob's dream: "The angels ascend and descend and their sympathetic presence makes sweeter our participation in the austere sacrifice."[89]

St Bernard had a vision of the holy angels standing by his monks in choir, and judging the attentiveness with which they sang the Divine Office.[90] He saw what we believe, namely, that, when here below we worship and praise God, we join in communion with the ninefold hierarchy, indeed with the Queen of Angels herself and all the blessed on high. As King David says, in words echoed by St Benedict in the Holy Rule, "in the sight of the angels will I sing to Thee" (Ps 137:2).[91] At the monastery of Heiligenkreuz in Austria this verse is given a beautiful expression: in the choir stalls, above the monks' heads, are images of the saints with open mouths, and between the saints are angels with musical instruments. The Cistercians sing the praises of God to the accompaniment of an angelic orchestra.

Some monks of past times thought that the chants of the Divine Office were composed by the angels. According to his biographer, St Dunstan, poet and musician as well as bishop and monk, received his melodies from "the citizens of the land of blessedness." They

---

89   A Benedictine Monk [Gérard Calvet, OSB], *The Sacred Liturgy* (London: The Saint Austen Press, 1999), 43. Compare Odilo Heiming, OSB: "[In celebrating the Eucharist] we ourselves perform the ministry of the angels. We are bodily liturgists, behind and in whom shines the liturgy of the bodiless: we are the icon of the angels. That is the teaching of the Great Entrance [in the Eastern liturgies]. But there is more. We have the privilege of sharing in the liturgy of liturgies, the liturgy of the blessed spirits: to sing the thrice-holy hymn to the thrice-holy God" ("Der Engel in der Liturgie" in *Die Engel in der Welt von heute*, ed. Theodor Bogler, OSB [Maria Laach: Ars Liturgica, 1957], 54f).
90   Cf. Conrad of Eberbach, *Exordium magnum cisterciense, sive narratio de initio cisterciensis ordinis*, ed. Bruno Griesser; CCCM 88.75.
91   "We believe that God is present everywhere, and that 'the eyes of the Lord in every place behold the good and the evil' (Prov 15:3), but let us especially believe this without any doubting when we are performing the Divine Office. Therefore, let us ever remember the words of the prophet: 'Serve ye the Lord in fear' (Ps 2:11); and again, 'Sing ye wisely' (Ps 46:8), and 'In the sight of the angels will I sing to thee' (Ps 137:2). Let us then consider how we ought to behave ourselves in the presence of God and His angels, and so sing the Psalms that mind and voice may be in harmony" (*The Rule of St Benedict in Latin and English*, ed. & trans. Abbot Justin McCann, OSB [London: Burns & Oates, 1952], ch. 19, 66–69).

invited him to join in their chanting and allowed him to transmit to other men the memory of what he had heard from on high.[92] Now pure spirits do not have vocal cords, and so, strictly speaking, cannot sing. However, just as they speak, according to St Thomas, by illuminating the minds of those beneath them,[93] so they can be said to sing through the high perfection of their adoration of God. In any case, both in Sacred Scripture and throughout the history of the Church, when Divine Providence makes the angels perceptible to men, singing is often the sign of their presence. The Church takes the cry of the Seraphim, the threefold *Sanctus* heard by the prophet (cf. Is 6:1ff), to be a song and repeats it in her liturgy. The angels sing *Gloria in excelsis Deo* above the frosty fields of Bethlehem (cf. Lk 2:14) to announce that the Father's eternal Son is born, in time and human nature, of a Virgin most pure. A schola of angels enters the cell of St Chad to tell him he is soon to die, and seven days later, with the soul of his already glorified brother, they come to take him home to heaven.[94]

The singing of the Psalms, said St Pius X, citing his predecessor Urban VIII, is the continuation on earth of the hymn sung in heaven before the throne of God and the Lamb.[95] According to Pope Pius XII, it was the divine Word himself who, "by assuming human nature, introduced into this earthly exile a hymn that is sung in the heavenly realm through all eternity. He unites to himself the whole human race and with it sings this hymn to the praise of God."[96] In His divine nature, Christ our Lord is the creator of the angels, and even in His human nature He is their Head, influencing them somewhat as He does men.[97] Therefore, when God the Son, eternally begotten of the Father, is born of the Blessed Virgin in time and humanity, He makes heard on this lowly earth the true music of the spheres, the canticles that echo through heaven in

---

92 Bridfert of Ramsey, *Sancti Dunstani vita*, cap. 5, PL 139.1443.
93 Cf. *ST* 1a q. 107, a. 1.
94 St Bede the Venerable, *Historia ecclesiastica* lib. 4, cap. 3; PL 95.177BD.
95 Cf. St Pius X, Apostolic Constitution *Divino afflatu* (November 1, 1911); AAS 3 (1911), 633.
96 Encyclical Letter *Mediator Dei* (November 20, 1947); AAS 39 (1947), 473.
97 Cf. *ST* 3a q. 8, a. 4.

adoration of the Most Holy Trinity: *Gloria in excelsis Deo, et in terra pax hominibus bonae voluntatis; Sanctus, sanctus, sanctus Dominus Deus Sabaoth.* Through Him, with Him, and in Him, the angels' song, first broadcast on Christmas night, continues every day in the sacred liturgy of His Mystical Body and Bride: in the Divine Office, and even more perfectly in the Holy Sacrifice of the Mass.

"BY CHARITY, NOT SERVITUDE": THE VENERATION OF THE ANGELS

However great their intellect and love, angels are mere creatures, and so, as the Apostle reminds us, we must not give them the adoration due to God alone (cf. Col 2:18, Apoc 22:9). "We honor them," says St Augustine, "by charity, not servitude."[98] However, Sacred Scripture also offers proof of the lesser honor due to glorified personal creatures. Outside the city of Jericho, Joshua venerates the angel who appears to him with a drawn sword and tells him: "I am prince of the host of the Lord, and now I am come" (Josh 5:14). Daniel falls on his face before the archangel Gabriel (cf. Dan 8:17). In the book of Tobias, Raphael reveals himself to be "one of the seven holy angels who present the prayers of the saints and enter into the presence of the glory of the Holy One" (Tobit 12:15). St John sees the angelic thurifer offering up the prayers of all the saints on the golden altar in front of the throne of God (cf. Apoc 8:3). Thus the prophets and apostles encourage us not only to venerate the angels, but to invoke them and ask their prayers. The prayers to angels most commonly used by Catholics are the prayer to St Michael, which, according to the command of Pope Leo XIII, is recited with other prayers after Low Mass,[99] and the prayer to one's guardian angel.[100]

---

98   St Augustine, *De vera religione* cap. 55, n. 110; PL34.170.

99   "Saint Michael the Archangel, defend us in battle; be our protection against the wickedness and snares of the devil. May God rebuke him, we humbly pray, and do thou, O Prince of the heavenly host, by the power of God, cast into hell Satan and all the evil spirits who prowl about the world seeking the ruin of souls" (to be found, in various translations, in most hand missals of the *Missale romanum* of 1962).

100   "Angel of God, my guardian dear, to whom God's love commits me here, ever this day be at my side, to light and guard, to rule and guide."

CONSOLING THE MARTYRS:
THE ANGELS IN THE LIVES OF THE SAINTS

The angelic intervention that the Church prays for in her *Ritual* the saints of every age experience in their sufferings and prayers.

> Angels come and console the martyrs in their prisons, and even heal their wounds, like so many good Samaritans; angels are seen taking care of the bodies of the Christian athletes, which the persecutor had thrown out to ignominious neglect; angels feed the hermits, and manifest to the early monastic lawgivers what is wise and what is excessive in Christian asceticism; they help the solitary to overcome his terrors at the sight of the solitudes filled with evil presences; they give warnings of the approaching death of some lonely servant of God, and they are seen carrying to heaven the soul of many a saint ... an angel girds the loins of St Thomas Aquinas with the mysterious *cingulum* of perfect chastity.... Angels are heard alternating with monks in divine psalmody in many a medieval abbey, when the brethren were in need of encouragement during the painful vigil of a cold winter night.[101]

When St Nicholas of Myra was dying, he asked our Lord to send him His angels, "and inclining his head he saw the angels come to him, where he knew well that he should depart, and began this holy Psalm, *In te Domine speravi* unto *in manus tuas*."[102] When the plague struck Rome, St Gregory the Great carried the icon of the Mother of God, health of the people of Rome, in a procession of penitence. When at last the air became clean, he heard the voice of angels singing *Regina caeli laetare*, "Joy to thee, O Queen of Heaven," to which he added the words, *Ora pro nobis Deum, alleluia*, "Pour for us to God thy prayer." At the same time he saw, on the top of Hadrian's Mausoleum, an angel

---

The Raccolta: Or Collection of Indulgenced Prayers and Good Works, edited by Ambrose St John, Cong. Orat., new edition (London: Burns & Oates, 1915), 267.

101 Vonier, *Teaching*, 257.

102 Jacob de Voragine, *The Golden Legend*, trans. William Caxton, ed. George V. O'Neill, SJ (Cambridge: The University Press, 1914), 69.

sheathing his sword; thanks to the intervention of the Mother
of God, Queen of Angels, the divine punishment had ceased.[103]

FREELY CREATED BY GOD:
UNDERSTANDING THE EXISTENCE OF THE ANGELS

Starting with the evidence of our senses, our minds by their
own light cannot with certainty know there are persons entirely
immaterial and unseen. There is nothing absolutely necessary or
self-evident about the existence of the angels; they have their
being by the utterly free act of the Creator. However, as we
think about the different levels of being and function among the
creatures that we perceive with our senses, we can infer with
high probability the existence of entirely spiritual creatures.[104]
The supreme Spirit that is God has created bodily creatures of
different kinds. There are material things without life (such as
pebbles on the beach), but also material things with life, whether
vegetative (such as dahlias in the garden) or sensitive (such as Spot
in his kennel). Finally, as the crown of the corporeal order, there
is man, made up of spirit as well as matter, "the swinging-wicket
set," as the poet says, "between the Unseen and Seen."[105] Now St
Thomas argues that, if man's intellect were the peak of the created
order, the only thing made to God's image, the world would be
incomplete, because a more perfect likeness to God would be
missing; we would then have creatures who understand, but only
at a very lowly level, in dependence on the body. For the order
of creation to be complete, for the greater likeness to be achieved,
there should be creatures who can understand, somewhat as God
understands, without dependence on the body.[106]

In the ancient world those philosophers who did not understand
what understanding was, the materialists who mixed up sense and
intellect, thought the only things that exist are what can be perceived with the senses or pictured by the imagination — in other

---

103   *The Golden Legend*, 133.
104   See above on the philosophical angelology of the pagan Greeks.
105   Francis Thompson, "Any Saint," in *Poems of Francis Thompson*, 183.
106   Cf. *ST* 1a q. 50, a. 1.

words, bodies.[107] Among the Jews, this was the root of the error of the Sadducees, who claimed there was neither angel nor soul (cf. Acts 23:8). Denial of the angels' existence, today as in the age of the apostles, derives from a failure to grasp the dignity of the human intellect. Once we have accepted the existence in man of a rational spiritual soul, which is but one part of the nature of man, we must at least admit the possibility of higher and simpler creatures with an entirely spiritual nature, intellects without bodies.

Angels are God's creatures, for everything that is not God is a creature of God. Nothing that is not God exists through itself, by necessity. God, and He alone, exists through Himself, by His very nature. All other things participate in existence, but God is existence, *ipsum esse per se subsistens*. Whatever is not God, including the mighty spirits we call angels, receives existence from God as a gift; the angels are His creatures.[108] As much as the lilies of the valley or the larks ascending in the sky, the citizens of the world invisible cry out, "We did not make ourselves."[109]

"BEYOND THE RANGE OF MORTAL MIND":
THE NUMBER OF THE ANGELS

Dante is dazzled by the vastness of the invisible world of the angels.

> The angelic nature in number doth extend
> so far beyond the range of mortal mind,
> no tongue or thought has ever reached the end.[110]

Dante echoes the amazement of the prophet and the apostle. Daniel sees "thousands and thousands" of angels ministering to the Ancient of Days (cf. Dan 7:10). In his own vision, St John gives the same number (cf. Apoc 5:11). Blessed Denys the Areopagite concedes that earthly mathematics cannot cope with

---

107 See 23f above.
108 Cf. *ST* 1a q. 61, a. 1 (on the angels as creatures); *ST* 1a q. 44, a. 1 (on God as the efficient cause of all things); 1a q. 4, a. 2 (God as *ipsum esse per se subsistens*).
109 Cf. St Augustine, *Confessiones* lib. 9, cap. 10, n. 25; PL 32.774.
110 *Paradiso* 29, 130–132; Sayers-Reynolds, 313.

the calculation: "So numerous indeed are the blessed armies of transcendent intelligent beings that they surpass the fragile and limited realm of our physical numbers."[111] St Thomas is of the same opinion: they "exist in an exceedingly great number, beyond all material multitude."[112] However, the number of the angels is not infinite, because, as Abbot Vonier says, following St Thomas, "an actually infinite series of created beings seems to involve metaphysical contradiction."[113] St Thomas says that the principle at stake here is that "the more perfect things are, the more they are created in excess for the perfection of the universe." In His loving wisdom, God makes what is best most abundant,[114] for such abundance is a fitting reflection of the infinite richness and unsurpassable beauty of the Trinitarian Godhead. "Why [asks Abbot Vonier] ... should we be scandalized if we hear it said that the angels differ as so many worlds, and yet are more numerous than the grains of sand on the seashore? Which is the more important work: to make a home for the ocean, or to represent adequately, in a created way, the glory of the Trinity?"[115]

RANK UPON RANK OF ANGELIC BLISS:
THE NINE ORDERS OF THE ANGELS

In Dante's vision, there are nine rings of fire round the Trinitarian central point. The nine rings stand for the three hierarchies of the angels, each with its own three orders. Of the lowest Dante says they are at *play*, for the holy angels exemplify *eutrapelia*,[116]

---

111   *De caelesti hierarchia*, cap. 14; PG 3.321A.
112   *ST* 1a q. 50, a. 3.
113   *The Human Soul*, in *The Collected Works of Abbot Vonier*, vol. 3, *The Soul and the Spiritual Life* (London: Burns & Oates, 1953), 175. "Every multitude existing in nature is created, and everything created comes under a clear intention of the Creator, for no agent does anything without some purpose. So everything created comes under a certain number. Therefore, it is impossible for an actually infinite multitude to exist, even accidentally. But a *potentially* infinite multitude is possible, because the increase of multitude follows upon the division of magnitude; since the more a thing is divided, the greater number of things result" (St Thomas, *ST* 1a q. 7, a. 4).
114   Cf. *ST* 1a q. 50, a. 3.
115   *The Human Soul*, 176.
116   Cf. *ST* 2a2ae q. 168, aa. 3 & 4.

the virtue of moderate playfulness; there is no toil in Paradise.[117] Blessed Denys and St Gregory rank the orders in slightly different ways: Seraphim, Cherubim, Thrones; Dominations, Virtues, Powers; Principalities, Archangels, and Angels (Denys); Seraphim, Cherubim, Thrones, Dominations, Principalities, Powers, Virtues, Archangels, and Angels (Gregory).[118] Both orderings, says St Thomas, as always reluctant to play off Father against Father, have something to be said for them; both can cite St Paul in support.[119] Dante follows the Areopagite rather than the great pope. He tells us that, when St Gregory finally saw the angels as they are, he accepted his mistake with that good humor with which the blessed are blessed:

> When Dionysius with ardent zest
>   pondered these orders of angelic bliss,
>   he named in this way, the true and best;
>
> But Gregory parted then differed over this,
>   and when his eyes were opened on this scene
>   he smiled to see how he had gone amiss.[120]

The angels are a multitude, not a mob. Divine Wisdom has organized its hosts in *hierarchies*. For Dante and Thomas, as for the Areopagite and all of Tradition, hierarchy is the handprint of the Creator. Hierarchy means "sacred principality."[121] Now God is the "prince," the ruler, of the principality of all His creatures, and beneath Him, in every work of His hands, there is a ranking in rule and dependence: in the Church, in human society, and the human body, in animals and plants, and above all in the invisible world of the angels. The reason is that hierarchy is a kind of order, and order is the imprint of intelligence. All things were created by God by His understanding and love, through His Wisdom and out of His Goodness. They therefore exist in order, an order that

---

117   ...*l'ultimo è d'angelici ludi* (*Paradiso* 28, 126).
118   Blessed Denys, *De caelesti hierarchia* cap. 7–cap. 9; PG 3.20B–261D; St Gregory, *Homiliae in evangelia*, liber 2, *Homilia* 34, n. 7; PL 76.1249D.
119   Cf. *ST* 1a q. 108, a. 6.
120   *Paradiso* 28, 130–135; Sayers-Reynolds, 304.
121   *ST* 1a q. 108, a. 1.

can be corrupted, of course, by creaturely wickedness. Moreover, within the hierarchical order that God has established, it is an unalterable law, according to Blessed Denys and St Thomas, that lower should be governed by higher.[122]

Since they are pure spirits, simple intelligences, the ordering of the angels can only be a ranking of their knowing: the higher angels give, the lower angels receive, the light of truth. "The theologians have clearly shown [says Blessed Denys] that the lower ranks of heavenly beings have in an orderly way received from their superiors whatever understanding they have of the works of God, whereas the higher ranks have been enlightened and initiated, so as far as is permitted, by the Godhead Itself."[123] No treasure of mind is hoarded away. In the three hierarchies, each made up of three orders or choirs, there is a descent in knowledge and understanding from more universal to less universal. The highest of the hierarchies (Seraphim, Cherubim, Thrones) knows the ideas (*rationes*) of things as they exist in the universal cause that is God; these angels, say Denys and Thomas, are "stationed on God's doorstep," and so they have a sense of God's view of things. The middle hierarchy (Dominations, Virtues, Powers) knows the ideas of things as they exist in the most universal created causes. The lowest hierarchy (Principalities, Archangels, Angels) knows the meaning of things in their individuality, as dependent on their proximate created causes; they see the details of the universe.[124]

For Dante, as for St Thomas, beatitude is essentially an act of the intellect, the face-to-face seeing of God: "Hence you can see that our beatitude/ is founded on the act of mind that sees,/ and not on love, which follows afterward."[125] Now the supernatural presupposes the natural, and so the supernatural hierarchy of

---

122 "God governs lower things through higher things, not because of a deficiency in His power but because of the abundance of His goodness; so that the dignity of causality may be imparted even to creatures" (*ST* 1a q. 22, a. 3).
123 *De caelesti hierarchia* cap. 7, n. 3; PG 3.209A.
124 *ST* 1a q. 108, a. 1.
125 *Paradiso* 28, 109–11; Esolen, 304–5. "Beatitude or happiness (*felicitas*) consists substantially and principally in an act of the intellect rather than in an act of the will" (*SCG* lib. 3, cap. 26, n. 11).

knowledge builds upon a natural ranking in intellect. "If angels differ in grace," says Abbot Vonier, "it is because they differ in nature, grace being granted to them according to the capacity of their nature."[126]

In St Gregory's interpretation, the names of the angelic orders tell us what they do. For example, the Angels announce little things, Archangels the greatest of the mysteries; Virtues work miracles; the Powers repel the demons; the Principalities rule the good spirits; and so on. Blessed Denys the Areopagite takes a different line: the names signify spiritual perfections, the qualities the angels possess. For example, the name "Seraphim," according to Denys and Thomas, expresses not just the charity of these exalted spirits, but its excess.[127] Dante calls them "pious flames" (*furchi pii*).[128] Just as fire moves upwards, so the Seraphim soar incessantly up to God. Flames penetrate hidden corners, and these angels, the highest ranking of all, "ignite a similar fervor in those below them and utterly purify them by the flame of love." Just as fire is a cause of light, so the Seraphim "have an inextinguishable light with them and perfectly enlighten others,"[129] bringing light by spiritual fire to the ones below them in the hierarchy. "The name 'Cherubim' signifies their power to know and see God, to receive the highest gifts of His light, to contemplate the beauty of the Godhead in its primal power, to be filled with the gift that makes one wise, and to share it ungrudgingly with the spirits of the second rank as an outpouring of the wisdom received."[130] As regards the operation of Providence, the highest hierarchy considers the end of all things in God; the middle one deals with the general plan, the strategy for achieving what needs to be done

---

126 Vonier, *Teaching*, 267. "Gratuitous gifts were given to the angels, according to the capacities of their natural endowments, which is not the case with men" (*ST* 1a q. 108, a. 4).

127 *ST* 1a q. 108, a. 5, ad 5.

128 *Paradiso* 9, 77; Esolen, 92–93.

129 *ST* 1a q. 108, a. 5, ad 5. St Bernard says that "the Seraphim, totally ablaze with the divine fire, set all things ablaze, so that every citizen [of the heavenly City] may be burning and shining lamps, burning with charity, shining with knowledge" (*De consideratione* lib. 5, cap. 4, n. 8; PL 182.792B).

130 *De caelesti hierarchia* cap. 7, n. 1; PG 3.205C.

to attain the end; while the lowest has the function of carrying things out.[131] According to St Bernard, each of the nine choirs of angels reflects a particular perfection of God.[132]

But, while there is hierarchy among God's creatures on earth, in heaven, and in hell,[133] there is no hierarchy in God Himself, the coequal, coeternal, and consubstantial Trinity. There is the natural order of the Divine Processions, the Son from the Father and the Holy Spirit from the Father and the Son, but no hierarchical order: none of the Persons is greater or less, none before or after. "God forbid," says St Thomas, "that we should attribute [hierarchical order] to the divine persons."[134]

→←

THE VERY EXISTENCE OF THE ANGELS, THE magnitude of their numbers beyond counting, and their ordering in hierarchies of pure light should move us to admiration of the brilliance of Eternal Wisdom and the generosity of Eternal Love manifested and communicated in these effects of Eternal Power.

> Now you can see [says Beatrice] the liberality
> and high magnificence of the eternal Power,
> pieced out among so many mirrors made,
>
> Remaining in Himself One, as before.[135]

---

131 Cf. *ST* 1a q. 108, a. 6.
132 Cf. *De consideratione* lib. 5, cap. 4, n. 10; PL 182. 793D–794A; *In cantica canticorum, sermo* 19, n. 6; PL 183. 865CD.
133 "If we look at the angelic orders as regards what is of nature, then the demons still exist in orders, because, as Denys says, they did not lose their natural endowments" (*ST* 1a q. 109, a. 1).
134 *ST* 1a q. 108, a. 1; cf. 1a q. 42, aa. 3 & 6.
135 *Paradiso* 29, 142–45; Esolen, 316–17.

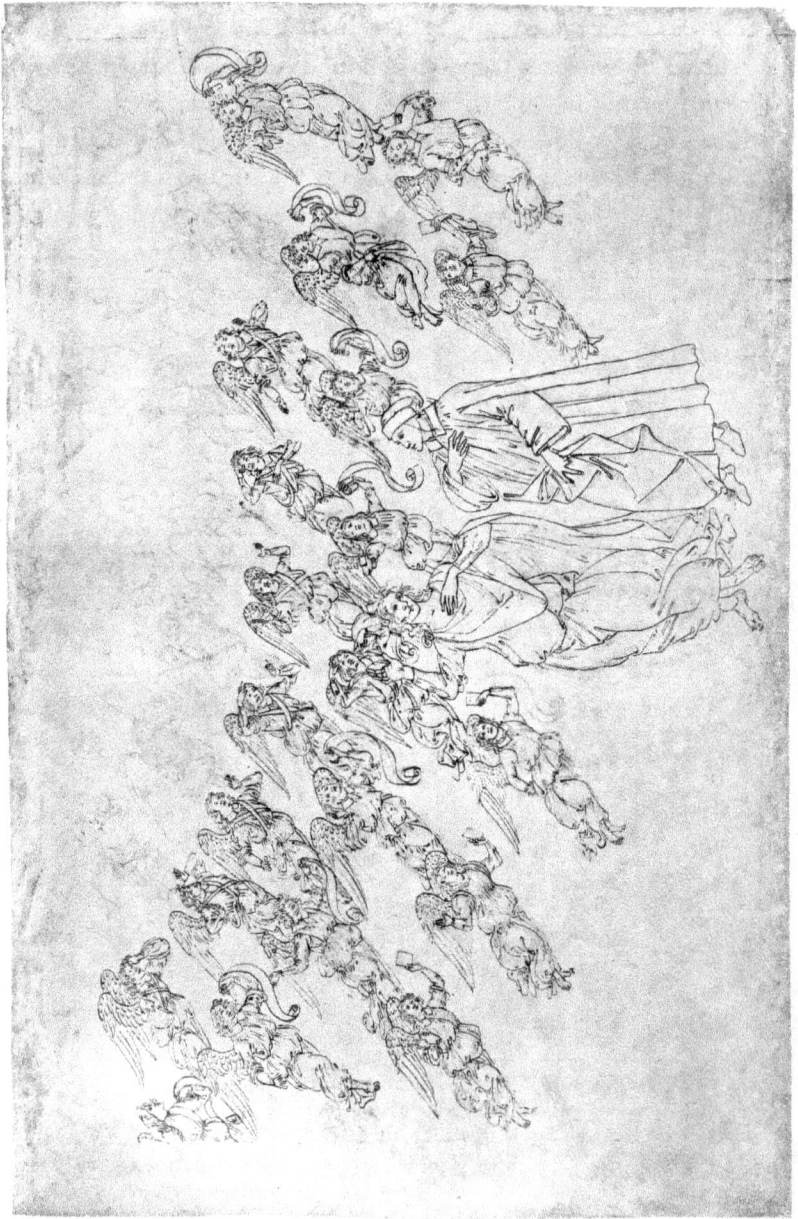

BOTTICELLI, PARADISO 29

2

SPIRITS · WHO
KNOW · AND · LOVE

THE NATURE OF THE ANGELS

Not to gain any good for Himself,
  which cannot be, but that His splendor,
  shining back, might say, "I subsist."

In His eternity, beyond time,
  beyond all confinement, as it pleased Him,
  opened up into new loves the Eternal Love.[1]

D
ANTE IN PARADISE HAS MUCH TO
learn, and Beatrice much to teach, not least about
the holy angels in heaven. In Botticelli's drawing of
Canto 28 the poet gazes upward, shielding his eyes with his
hand, for the dancing orders transmit a light too bright for him
to bear.[2] Beatrice reminds Dante that God created the angels, as
He created all things, for the love of His goodness; not to "gain" it,
because it is infinitely perfect, but to communicate and diffuse it
in "new loves."[3] In the relative simplicity and spirituality of their

---

1   *Paradiso* 29, 13–18; author's translation. The speculations of the Schoolmen
fall far short of the glorious reality: "Because on earth, in your schools,/ they
teach that the angelic nature/ is such that it understands, remembers, and wills,/
I will say more, that you may see the pure/ truth that is down below confused,/
in their equivocating readings" (*Paradiso* 29, 70–75; author's translation). On
memory in the angels, see *ST* 1a q. 54, a. 5. Memory can be attributed to the
angels in the Augustinian sense of mind, but not as part of a sensitive soul.
2   Drawing of *Paradiso* 28; Botticelli, p. 211.
3   "God, who of all things is the first agent, does not act as acquiring
something by His action, but as lavishing something by His action" (*SCG*
lib. 3, cap. 18). "Some things act and are acted upon. They are imperfect
agents; even in acting they intend to acquire something. But the First Agent,
who is purely an agent, does not act to acquire some end; He intends only
to communicate His perfection, which is His goodness" (*ST* 1a q. 44, a. 4).

being, the angels share in and shine back the splendor of their Creator, and return His love, with greater perfection than men do in their complexity and bodiliness. St John Paul II sums up Tradition's understanding when he says: "God, who is absolutely perfect Spirit, is reflected especially in the spiritual beings who by nature, that is, by reason of their spirituality, are nearer to Him than material creatures, and who constitute, as it were, the closest 'circle' to the Creator."[4] This is the truth Dante expresses by the image of the nine rings of fire speeding round the divine and central point.

This chapter is about the nature of the angels, what God has made the angels to be, and what He has equipped them to do. Without some knowledge of the angelic nature, we cannot understand how the good angels help us and the bad angels hurt us, nor how an angel can sin and remain forever fixed in his rebellion against God without chance of repentance or hope of redemption.

"WHO MAKES HIS ANGELS SPIRITS":
THE BODILESS POWERS OF HEAVEN

Can we know what the angels are? It would seem not. The human soul, united to the body, is lowest in the scale of intellectual substances and least in power. The proper object of our minds in their natural state is the essence of sensible things abstracted from the data of the senses.[5] Now angels are pure spirits, and so we cannot perceive them by our senses and form an adequate image of them. Therefore, by its natural powers "the human soul, united to this kind of body, [cannot] apprehend separate substances in the sense of knowing *what* they are."[6] However, Divine Revelation teaches us *that* the angels are "spirits," intellectual creatures who know and love. Therefore, arguing by analogy, we can apply to them what we know of our own intellects, while removing from

---

4   General Audience address, September 7, 1986.
5   Cf. St Thomas Aquinas, *Sententia libri De anima*, lib. 3, lect. 8.
6   St Thomas, *Sententia libri Metaphysicae*, lib. 2, lect. 1, n. 285. "An angel cannot properly speaking be defined, for we do not know what he is, but he can be made known by certain negations and notifications" (*Quaestio disputata de anima* a. 7, ad 16).

them the inconveniences of having a mind united to a body.

The Byzantine liturgy refers to the angels as "the honored, *bodiless* powers of Heaven."[7] This is the first truth to understand: the angels do not have bodies, even of the most subtle kind. As proof, St Thomas quotes the words of David in the Psalm: "who makes His angels *spirits*" (Ps 103:4).[8] What, then, of St John Damascene's claim that angels are dense and material in relation to the incomparable God?[9] According to St Thomas, Damascene's point is not that angels have bodies, but that, considered in contrast to their Creator, who is infinite simplicity and spirit, they appear to be material. In a certain sense, bodiless creatures stand midway between the immaterial God and bodily creatures such as ourselves. Now the middle compared with one extreme seems like the opposite extreme: tepid tea, compared with a freshly boiled cup, strikes the early riser as positively cold. That is why, concludes Thomas, someone might think that angels, matched against the infinite immaterial God, have some kind of matter or body.[10]

The angels do not have bodies, nor do we find in them the composition of form and matter.[11] The argument that a form without matter would be pure act, something no creature can ever be, does not stand up. The immaterial angelic form is still related to its *existence* as potency to act.[12] Compared with man in his improbable complexity of flesh and spirit, the angels in their pure spirituality seem simple, but they are not absolutely and unchangeably simple, without any composition at all.[13] God alone is without the compo-

---

7   *Divine Liturgy*, 51.

8   Cf. *ST* 1a q. 50, a. 1, *sed contra*.

9   *De fide orthodoxa* lib. 2, cap. 3; PG 94.868A. St Bernard is uncertain: "The Fathers seem to have had different opinions about this matter, nor is it clear to me that I should teach otherwise, and I confess I do not know" (*In Cantica canticorum, Sermo* 5, n. 7; PL 183.801B). As part of its reaction against Scholasticism, the "Platonic Theology" of the Renaissance, including among its heirs John Milton, "believed all created spirits to be corporeal." This turn in philosophical angelology is discussed by C. S. Lewis in *A Preface to* Paradise Lost (London: Oxford University Press, 1960), 108ff.

10   Cf. *ST* 1a q. 50, a. 1, ad 1.

11   Cf. *ST* 1a q. 50, a. 2.

12   Cf. *ST* 1a q. 50, a. 2, ad 3.

13   "A spiritual creature is simple in its essence, yet there is still a twofold

sition of existence and essence. He is the essentially self-subsistent being (*ipsum esse per se subsistens*).[14] The true God, who revealed Himself to Moses as "I am who am," exists *by essence*, whereas His creatures, including the angels, exist *by participation*, by receiving their being as a gift from God; their shared and imperfect being is caused by the unique First Being who exists in the most perfect way.[15] Angels are dependent, limited, caused beings, sharers and receivers of existence, the creatures of God.[16]

Although by nature the angels do not possess bodies, they can, for the ministry God gives them, assume bodies when they appear to men, as we learn from three of them enjoying the hospitality of Abraham (Gen 18:1ff), St Raphael in the form of "a beautiful young man" accompanying Tobias (cf. Tob 5:5), and an angel with "a countenance like lightning and raiment as snow" rolling back the stone from the tomb (cf. Mt 28:2f; Mk 16:5; Lk 24:4; Jn 20:12). According to St Thomas, there are two reasons for this temporary deployment of bodily form:

> Angels need an assumed body, not for themselves, but for us, so that, by conversing familiarly with men, they may manifest the fellowship of intellect that men hope to have with them in the life to come. Moreover, the fact that angels assumed bodies in the Old Testament was an indication and foreshadowing that the Word of God would assume a human body, for all the appearances in the Old Testament were ordered to the appearance in which the Son of God appeared in the flesh.[17]

Angels do not inform their temporary bodies the way the rational soul informs the human body, as if angel and body were the constituents of a composite nature. The angel is complete and

---

composition in the spiritual creature, namely, that of essence with existence, and that of substance with accidents" (Seventh of the Approved Theses of Thomistic Philosophy, Decree of the Sacred Congregation of Studies, July 27, 1914; DS 3607. Cf. St Thomas, *De spiritualibus creaturis*, a. 1).

14   Cf. *ST* 1a q. 3, a. 4; q. 4, a. 2.
15   Cf. *ST* 1a q. 4, a. 2; q. 44, a. 1.
16   Cf. *ST* 1a q. 61, a. 1. See 52 above.
17   *ST* 1a q. 51, a. 2, ad 1.

entire in his pure spirituality. His assumed body is just a tool for getting a job done: communicating a message to the embodied minds of men. Pure spirits are not capable of the acts of bodily life, as St Raphael explains to Tobias: "I seemed indeed to eat and drink with you, but I use an invisible meat and drink that cannot be seen by men" (Tob 12:19). However, as we noticed earlier,[18] the angelic visitations in the Old Testament are a promise of eternal beatitude to be spent in the company of the angels, and a prophecy of the Incarnation, by which God the Son unites a complete human nature to himself, a body animated by a rational soul, and really eats and sleeps, suffers and dies and rises again, in the body He has made His very own. Angels take up bodies and put them down again. But what God takes, He keeps. In the body born of the Virgin Mary, crucified and risen, the eternal Son ascended into heaven, in that body He sits at the Father's right hand, and in the body, still bearing its glorious scars, He will come again to judge the living and the dead.

Angels are not bodies and therefore cannot be in places in a bodily way. Bodies are in places by "measurable quantity": their measurements correspond to the measurements of the places they occupy. Uncle Joe is obliged to fly Business, because there is too much of Uncle Joe to fit into a seat in Economy. A body in a place is contained and circumscribed by it; to draw a line round the body is to draw a line round its place in the world. A body can therefore only *be* in one place at a time. By contrast, angels are wherever they apply their power.[19] However, since their power is creaturely and limited, they *operate* in one definite place rather than another. God alone, the universal cause, is in all places, because all things in all places depend upon His infinite power.[20]

---

18 See 35f above.
19 Cf. *ST* 1a q. 52, a. 1.
20 Cf. *ST* 1a q. 52, a. 2.

STARS OF THE INVISIBLE WORLD:
THE ANGELS AS SPECIES

When we count human persons, we count heads. How do you count angelic persons, who are singularly lacking in heads? They have no heads, no bodies, no matter to mark off one of them from another. When two bodily things belong to the same species, for example, two beech trees, we can still distinguish them by their matter (and thus their location, size, health, etc.). This beech tree is what that beech tree is, and the two look much the same, but this tree stands on the left-hand side of the drive, with its own foliage, and that tree is on the other side, with a separate set of branches. Now angels are pure spirits, simple forms without matter or means of individuation. Therefore, St Thomas concludes, they cannot be individuals within a single species.[21] In fact, he says it is impossible for two angels to be of the same kind. Now since God, who is truth and the source of all truth, cannot make a contradiction true, it follows that even He cannot create two angels within the same species.[22] The angel has comrades in the orders and hierarchies, but the angel knows nothing of uniformity or kinship. Angel differs from angel as lion differs from eagle. Each angel, says Kenelm Foster, "in and by himself realizes the fullness of his angelhood."[23]

The human mind cannot fail to be dazzled by the thought of angelic uniqueness. "Every angel is a separate species [writes Abbot Vonier], being, as it were, a world to himself, a star in the angelic world, holding in the universe a place of unique importance, in fact being indispensable to its completeness. If he were not just where he is, the world would not be complete; there would be a gap."[24] The phrase "star in the angelic world" is telling. Blessed Denys the Carthusian compares the angels, each of his own kind, to the heavenly bodies in their differentness. He makes the point

21 Cf. *ST* 1a q. 50, a. 4.
22 *De spiritualibus creaturis* a. 8; *ST* 1a q. 75, a. 7.
23 Kenelm Foster, OP, in St Thomas Aquinas, *Summa theologiae*, vol. 9, 1a qq. 50–64 (London: Blackfriars, 1968), 23n.
24 Vonier, *Collected Works*, 180.

in his commentary on the Advent hymn *Conditor alme siderum.*

> "Dear Maker of the stars of night" can also be under-
> stood of the spiritual stars, that is, of all the holy angels
> and citizens above, of whom the Lord speaks in the
> book of Job: "Where wast thou when I laid the foun-
> dations of the earth, when the morning stars and all
> the sons of God made a joyful melody?" (Job 38:4, 7).
> Clearly, the Empyrean Heaven, especially the Church
> Triumphant, is adorned and shines with these stars in
> a more beautiful way than do the revolving heavens
> with their visible stars, planets, and perfections.[25]

Although Scripture and Tradition give only four of the angels
personal names (the archangels Michael, Gabriel, and Raphael,
and the fallen angel Satan), we must not think of any of them
as lacking personhood. On the contrary, the angels, each in his
specific uniqueness, are more perfectly personal than men are.
"Man [writes Denys the Carthusian] subsists in the parts that make
him up, the angel in his simple nature. Man thinks discursively;
the angel understands by simple intuition. Man is individuated
by matter; the angelic nature is determined out of itself, neither
depending on nor needing the support of matter."[26] Our holy
angelic helpers and our wicked angelic tempters are not impersonal
forces, but living persons, with the faculties of intellect and will.

THROUGH THE AGES OF AGES:
THE ENDLESSNESS OF THE ANGELS

The angels have a beginning but no end. Only what is made
up of form and matter can fall apart. But angels are simple forms,
without matter. Therefore, they lack the wherewithal for dissolu-
tion. They last forever; their nature is immortal.[27] Age does not
weary them, nor do the years condemn. They do not fall sick
and grow old, nor do they decline into death — the only death to

---

25 *Expositio hymnorum aliquot ecclesiasticorum;* DCOO 35.24D–25A.
26 *Creaturarum in ordine ad Deum consideratio theologica* a. 17; DCOO
34.113D–113A.
27 Cf. *ST* 1a q. 50, a. 5.

which angels have ever succumbed is the spiritual death of eternal deprivation of the Beatific Vision. Such was the fate of Lucifer and his gang after they failed their testing by God.[28] The angels are everlasting, but not eternal in the strict sense.[29] Eternity is not only endlessness, continuing to exist forever, but also beginninglessness and the freedom from succession, from all shifting from past into present and future. In God alone do we find such eternity, what Boethius calls "the completely simultaneous and perfect possession of unending life."[30] Anscar Vonier explains: "Eternity is the measure of God's existence; it implies negation, not only of an end but also of a beginning; it implies, moreover, immutability of every kind, even immutability in intellect and will: such immutability or eternity is possessed by God alone."[31]

The angels, therefore, are no more strictly eternal than they are altogether unchanging. They exist in what the Schoolmen call the *aevum*, "the age," which is a "participated eternity."[32] Angelic life is not measured by the tick of the clock, the relentless recording of change and decay in this material world. But there is still some change, a sort of succession, in the angels, in what happens to their ideas and acts of will: they are unchangeable in being, but changeable in understanding, in choosing, and in the places in which they operate.[33] By a mistaken judgement and a bad choice, some of the angels fell into eternal damnation, the worst of all changes.

Even though the angels will never cease to exist, they did begin to exist; they were created when everything else was created. Their *world invisible* is part of the universe, not a private cosmos of their own. "The good of the universe [argues St Thomas] is the ordered relationship of things to each other. Now no part is perfect when separated from the whole. It is therefore improbable

---

28 In *ST* 1a q. 64, a. 2, St Thomas quotes Damascene: "As death is to human beings, so their fall was to the angels" (cf. *De fide orthodoxa* lib. 2, cap. 4; PG 94.877).
29 Cf. *ST* 1a q. 61, a. 2.
30 Boethius, *De consolatione philosophiae*, lib. 5, prosa 6; PL 63.858A.
31 Vonier, *Teaching*, 261.
32 Cf. *Sent.* lib. 1, d. 8, q. 2, a. 2. The *aevum* is a mean between God's eternity and earthly time (cf. *ST* 1a q. 10, a. 5).
33 Cf. *ST* 1a q. 10, a. 5.

that God, whose 'works are perfect' (cf. Dt 35:4), would have created the angelic creature before other creatures."[34]

FINDING, NOT SEEKING: THE ANGELS' KNOWLEDGE

The angels are endowed with intellect: they have knowledge and understanding. Now to know something is to take it into oneself, somehow to *be* it. This red rose comes into my senses, into my eyes by its redness and into my nose by its fragrance. My imagination and memory register and preserve the impression made on my senses. My intellect takes hold of the nature of the rose. High in the sky, the physical sun lights up the rose, revealing its color and shape, and in my soul a spiritual sun, the "agent intellect," shines upon the sensory image of the rose, lighting up what is intelligible, the whatness of the rose, before passing it on, as an idea, to the "possible intellect," the receptive mind, for the task of actual understanding.[35] Human knowledge is a process of deepening intimacy with reality: the rose exists as a material and lovely thing in my garden, as a visual image in my eyes, as an idea in my mind. The senses, say Aristotle and Aquinas, *are* all sensible things, and the intellect is everything intelligible.[36] My mind can gather the whole universe into itself. The intellect is nothing if not catholic.

But whereas men work hard to attain knowledge, angels are always in possession of what they naturally know; they received it long ago with their existence and nature. The luminosity of things is present to the angel's mind, from the beginning, through the ideas poured into him by God.[37] There is no effort in the way the angels know and understand, no burning of the midnight oil

---

34   St Thomas, *ST* 1a q. 61, a. 3. St Thomas is careful to add in the same place that the contrary opinion is not heretical. St Gregory Nazianzen, whose "authority is so great that no one has presumed to calumniate his teaching," argued that the angels were created before the visible universe.

35   "Things are made present to the human mind as images (*species*). In the order of nature, they need to be made present to the senses; secondly, to the imagination; thirdly, to the possible intellect, which takes in the ideas (*species*) of things as abstracted from sense-images (*speciebus phantasmatum*) by the light of the agent intellect" (*ST* 2a 2ae q. 173, a. 2).

36   Cf. *Quaestiones de quolibet* 7, q. 1, a. 2.

37   Cf. *ST* 1a q. 55, aa. 1 & 2.

or peering into microscopes; as Fr Bonino says, in knowing, the angel "does not seek, he finds."[38] The angel is created with his knowledge, in complete independence of the material world; his ideas are innate. These angelic ideas, or intelligible species, are the first copy of the ideas in the mind of God, the first participation of the First Truth.[39] Now God communicates His ideas in two ways: by making them into existing realities, and by imparting them, still as ideas, to the minds of the angels. The angel cannot smell the rose that spreads its fragrance in my garden in the cool of evening, but from the beginning of his existence he has had the idea of the rose in his mind.[40]

KNOWING AND BEING

Angels have no bodies, no sense-organs, and therefore no sensitive knowledge. Their knowing is entirely intellectual, which is why they are called "intelligences."[41] What angels do is *understand*. And yet they are not the same thing as their actual understanding, because in no creature is activity, the actualizing of a power, really identical with its substance or essence.[42] Only God, who is pure act, *is* His own act of understanding, as He is His own act of being. If the actual understanding of an angel were its substance, it would be subsistent understanding, Intelligence itself, and then there would be only one of him, and he would be indistinguishable from God and other angels. If an angel were his own actual understanding, he would not exist, as we know he does exist, in a dazzling hierarchy of greater and less understanding, from mere Angels to the great Seraphim. Differences in rank denote differences of sharing, and sharing is the tell-tale sign of the real distinction in the creature between what it is and what it does. Even the highest of the Cherubim is not Intelligence itself, which

38 Bonino, 153.
39 "The angelic ideas are ... a participation in the divine ideas, by which God produces things." Reginald Garrigou-Lagrange OP, *La synthèse thomiste* (Paris: Desclee, 1946), 261.
40 Cf. *ST* 1a q. 56, a. 2.
41 Cf. *ST* 1a q. 54, a. 5.
42 Cf. *ST* 1a q. 54, a. 1.

is God.[43] The angels' understanding has a kind of infinity, because it can reach out to everything understandable, but its existence, which is created, is finite. Therefore, the actual understanding of the angel is not the same thing as its existence.[44] The angels differ in essence from men, their fellow creatures, but they differ still more radically, in essence and existence, from God, their Creator.[45] Even to the highest of the Seraphim, God can say what He once told St Catherine of Siena in a mystical locution: "You are [the one] who is not, whereas I am He Who Is."[46]

KNOWING BY INTUITION

Our natural way of thinking is by discursive reason: we feel our way through an argument step by step, making distinctions and connections as we move towards the conclusion. Sometimes, but only sometimes, we have a sudden flash of insight, and just *see* the truth and get the idea; we enjoy an *intuition* that reaches the heart of the matter without the preliminaries. The people we call geniuses, in music or mathematics or the detection of crime, seem in their own field to know naturally in this way. In the supernatural order, the act of contemplation, grounded in faith and love, is an "intuiting of simple truth."[47] Even the simplest of folk, children and the mentally handicapped, can display astonishing intuition of the mysteries of the faith through the Holy Spirit's gifts of wisdom and understanding.[48] Now what for us is naturally unusual and supernaturally occasional is for the angels the ordinary way of understanding; intuiting the truth is their natural style: "In the things they know naturally, they at once behold (*inspiciunt*) all things that can be known in

---

43 Cf. *ST* 1a q. 54, a. 1.
44 Cf. *ST* 1a q. 54, a. 2.
45 "He must be proclaimed as really and essentially distinct from the world." The First Vatican Council, Dogmatic Constitution *Dei Filius* on the Catholic Faith (1870), ch. 1; DS 3001. See 52 and 62 above.
46 Blessed Raymond of Capua, *The Life of St Catherine of Siena* (Rockford: TAN Books, 2003), 79.
47 Cf. *ST* 2a2ae q. 180, a. 3.
48 See Daniel-Ange, *Ton enfant, il crie la verité: Catechisme pour théologiens* (Paris: Fayard, 1983).

them."[49] The angels do not construct propositions by combining and distinguishing concepts, nor do they deploy syllogisms, though they understand such complexities of human thought with their native simplicity, just as they understand material things in the unfleshly style of pure spirits.[50] The angels do not study or conduct research; in one swift movement, like the flash of a rapier, their minds cut open the truth of things. The immediacy and penetration of their knowing explains why the tradition calls the angels intellectual rather than strictly rational creatures, for what is *intellegere* (*intus-legere*) if not reading your way into the innermost mystery of a thing?[51]

> We call [the angels] intellectual beings, for, even in our case, those things we grasp naturally and immediately are said to be understood (*intellegi*), and so we give the name "intellect" [or understanding] to our habitual capacity to grasp first principles. But human souls, which acquire knowledge of truth in a step-by-step way (*per quemdam discursum*), we call rational. This is because of the feebleness of intellectual light in them. If our souls had the fullness of intellectual light, as the angels do, they would comprehend at first glance the entire force of the principles, intuiting whatever could be derived from them by a syllogism.[52]

The substantial form of a material thing is its intelligibility: to know that something is a dog is to grasp, within all its furry materiality, its form, what makes it a dog, its dogginess. Now an angel is a form without matter, furry or otherwise, and therefore intelligible of himself. To be a pure form, a bodiless spirit, is to be self-knowing. Our human minds, working through the senses, are turned outwards to the material world, but the angelic mind,

---

49 *ST* 1a q. 58, a. 3.
50 Cf. *ST* 1a q. 58, a. 4.
51 "The intellect takes its name from the fact that it knows the inwardness of things, for to understand is, as it were, 'to read within.' The senses and the imagination know only the exterior accidents of things; only the intellect reaches the inwardness and essence of things" (St Thomas, *De veritate* q. 1, a. 12).
52 *ST* 1a q. 58, a. 3.

without senses, is turned inwards. He knows himself through himself, through his own substance, somewhat as God knows Himself.[53]

KNOWING THE ETERNAL GOD,
KNOWING THINGS IN TIME

Every angel, whether holy or fallen, has a natural knowledge of God. Such knowledge is different from the sublime supernatural knowledge that the blessed spirits enjoy in Heaven through their immediate vision of His essence. Nor is it like the natural knowledge we men attain when we prove God's existence through His likeness reflected in His creatures in the visible world (cf. Rom 1:20). The angels' natural knowledge of God stands in the middle between these two kinds of knowing, supernatural and natural. As in the Beatific Vision, they somehow know God in themselves, but, as men do, they know God through an image, which for them means the image of God in which they were created. The angel, unlike fallen man, never fails to perceive the dignity of his Godlike nature.[54] Through the ideas implanted in him at the beginning of his existence by God, the angel has a natural knowledge of all the other angels in their mind-dazzling multitude,[55] of material things,[56] and of particular things (not just universal causes), a knowledge they put to good use when they serve God in the governing of this world.[57]

Angels know with certainty future events that come by necessity from their causes (such as the rising of the sun tomorrow), and they know with high probability, and with greater perfection than any human being does, those future events which very often come from their causes (such as lung disease from heavy smoking).[58] However, the angels cannot by nature know future free events; such knowledge only God possesses, who, in the serenity of His

---

53   Cf. *ST* 1a q. 56, a. 1.
54   Cf. *ST* 1a q. 56, a. 3.
55   Cf. *ST* 1a q. 56, a. 2
56   Cf. *ST* 1a q. 57, a. 1.
57   Cf. *ST* 1a q. 57, a. 2.
58   Cf. *ST* 1a q. 57, a. 3.

ever-abiding Now, sees all that for us is past, present, or future.[59] That is why Isaiah says: "Show the things that are to come hereafter, and we shall know that ye are gods" (Is 41:23). When God, by an extraordinary grace, gives holy men, such as Padre Pio, the power to know the future, He does something so exceptional that it supplies us with a reason for recognizing the unrivalled supernatural dignity of His Church and her saints, a motive of credibility.

The angels' knowledge of our minds is strictly limited. Not even the highest of the Cherubim can discover by his native powers what I am going to do next, or what ideas are passing through my mind. Our souls, in their highest faculties of intellect and will, are a sanctuary Almighty God alone can enter. To Him all hearts are open, all desires known, but not to the angels. Of course, as we do less subtly and accurately, they can decipher our inward thoughts from the code of our outward actions, or from the clues they notice in our bodies (smiles or tears or sweating), or from the signals they find in our imagination, but they cannot hear what we are saying to ourselves in the inner temple of our hearts.[60]

Angels possess all their ideas from the beginning of their existence, but their ideas of human activity cause actual knowledge in their minds only when the ideas become realities in time. Kenelm Foster compares the angelic species to "a great critic's understanding of a great artist, while the latter is still in full career," such as John Steane on the singing of Elisabeth Schwarzkopf: he knows her capacities and achievements better than anyone, perhaps than the singer herself, but a new production of *Fidelio* may still offer him something new, if only the clearest demonstration hitherto of the diva's greatness. Foster goes on to say: "[The angelic species] does not give the angel exact knowledge of whatever has yet to be created. Why? Because the latter is still only potentially, not actually, representing that *species*. When it does begin to exist, the angel *recognizes* it. It conforms to his thought rather than *vice versa*."[61] The angels certainly grow in their knowledge of

---

59   Cf. *ST* 1a q. 57, a. 3.
60   Cf. *ST* 1a q. 57, a. 4.
61   Kenelm Foster, OP, in St Thomas Aquinas, *Summa theologiae*, vol. 9, 135n.

what can be known only by divine revelation: "Until the day of judgement new things are always being revealed by God to the highest of the angels concerning the ordering (*dispositionem*) of the world and especially the salvation of the elect. There is always something the higher angels can make known to the lower."[62]

KNOWLEDGE AND ERROR

Through the ideas of things with which they were created, angels see exactly what things are, and know everything that can be said about them, and so cannot fall into error.[63] The Lord God of truth is the informant of their minds, and He can make no mistake. The angels cannot be deceived about the nature of a thing, but the fallen angels do go wrong in the supernatural order:

> Good angels, who are upright in will, through their knowledge of what things are, never make a judgement about things in the natural order that is at odds with God's plan for the world, and so in the good angels there can be no falsehood or error. But the demons, because of the perversion of their will, have intellects divorced from Divine Wisdom, and so from time to time they make absolute judgements that take only natural conditions into account. In this respect, as regards things in the natural order, they are not deceived. But as regards supernatural matters, they can be deceived. For example, seeing a dead man, they presume he will not rise again, and seeing the man Christ they suppose He is not God.[64]

The demons in their pride are know-alls and bigots, but they are also eaten up with curiosity about the supernatural, and so they tempt the Lord Jesus, taunt and attack Him, to discover who He is.[65]

---

62 *ST* 1a q. 106, a. 4, ad 3.
63 *ST* 1a q. 58, a. 3.
64 *ST* 1a q. 58, a. 5.
65 See 135 below on the temptations of Christ.

MORNING AND EVENING KNOWLEDGE

In Genesis 1, Moses distinguishes between "morning" and "evening" of each of the six days of creation (cf. Gen 1:5ff). In his literal commentary on Genesis, St Augustine argues that these mornings and evenings are not periods of cosmic time, but perfections of angelic mind; after all, there could be no mornings and evenings in the literal sense, no gleam of sunrise or glow of sunset, before the sun itself had been created on the fourth day.[66] St Thomas adopts St Augustine's exegesis, and argues that what counts in the thinking of the sacred author is the idea of beginning within the idea of morning, and of end in the evening.

> Just as the morning is the beginning of the ordinary day and the evening its end, so the angel's knowledge of the primordial being of things is called "morning knowledge," and this is knowledge of things as they exist in the Word. But the knowledge of the being of the created thing, as it exists in its own nature, is called evening knowledge. For the being of things flows from the Word as from a primordial beginning, and this flow ends up in the existence that things have in their own nature.[67]

The angels' morning knowledge of the Word, and of creatures in Him, is the same thing as the Beatific Vision, the immediate seeing of the Word as He is in Himself, with the Father and the Holy Spirit, in the one essence of the Godhead. This glorious supernatural knowledge was merited by the angels when, by their first act of charity, they gave themselves to God, and so entered eternal bliss with Him.[68] They also know the Word by the powers of their nature in the sense of recognizing His likeness in their intellects; these sublimely logical creatures have a God-given resemblance to the uncreated Logos.

The fallen angels are deprived eternally of the Beatific Vision,

---

66   Cf. St Augustine, *De genesi ad litteram* lib. 4, cap. 22; PL 34.312; *De genesi ad litteram* lib. 4, cap. 26; PL 34.314.
67   *ST* 1a q. 58, a. 6.
68   Cf. *ST* 1a q. 62, a. 5.

of the immediate "morning" knowledge of the Word. Can we say, then, that they retain the twilight knowledge of evening? According to St Thomas, they do not.

> Creatures are dark compared with the excellence of divine light. Therefore, the knowledge of a creature in its proper nature is called evening knowledge, for in the evening darkness begins to fall, but there is still some light; when all light has gone, it is night. So even the knowledge of things in their proper nature, when it is directed to praise of the Creator, has something of the divine light, and can be called evening knowledge. If it is not directed to God, as is true of the demons, it is not called evening knowledge, but nocturnal knowledge.[69]

The minds of the demons are dark with night, not bright with light. They are the powers of darkness.

THE FLOW OF LIGHT

The use of the analogy of daylight for understanding mind and truth is common to the ancient Greek philosophers, the prophets and apostles, and the Fathers and Doctors of the Church. The philosophical reflection has its starting point in ordinary human experience. When we understand a thing, it seems to light up our minds, as the rays of the rising sun drive away the darkness, and we see where we are going. In a moment of sudden realization, we gasp, "It's suddenly *dawned* on me," and Duke Ellington confesses to the lady he loves, "Now that the stars are in your eyes, I'm beginning to see the light." Just as physical light causes an object to be actually visible to our eyes, so the spiritual light of man's agent intellect makes the data of the senses actually intelligible; that is, through the concept it has abstracted from them it causes knowledge in the possible intellect.[70] The intelligibility of reality is a kind of luminosity, the splendor of the truth. The intelligent are the bright, the very

---

69 *ST* 1a q. 64, a. 1, ad 3.
70 Cf. *SCG* lib. 2, cap. 59, n. 14.

intelligent the brilliant. Now, God, the first cause of all things, is the source of truth and therefore of all the light that dawns upon His creatures, in their capacities both to understand and to be understood, in the minds that understand and the things that are understood. The physical brightness of this world, the sunshine that brightens fields and flowers, is but a trace of the immaterial beams streaming forth from the Creator, the Father of lights (cf. Jas 1:17). [71]

> The glory of the One who moves all things
>> penetrates the universe with light,
>> more radiant in one part and elsewhere less.[72]

If the angels have the light of understanding, it is from God that they receive it. God, says Dante in the *Paradiso*, is the "sun of the angels."[73] He is the "threefold light,"[74] for within the uncreated life of the Trinitarian Godhead there is an eternal reflecting of "light from light" in the person of the Son and Word, the Image of the Father and "the radiance of the Father's glory" (*splendor paternae gloriae*), as the Ambrosian hymn puts it, echoing the Apostle (cf. Heb 1:3).[75] And the Son, too, with the

---

71   Did the clarity of the physical light in Greece contribute to the intellectual luminosity of her philosophers and their predilection for analogies of light? "Nor is it perhaps fanciful to think that the Greek light played a part in the formation of Greek thought. Just as the cloudy skies of northern Europe have nursed the huge, amorphous progeny of Norse mythology or German metaphysics, so the Greek light surely influenced the clear-cut conceptions of Greek philosophy." C. M. Bowra, *The Greek Experience* (London: Weidenfeld & Nicholson, 1957), 11.
72   *Paradiso* 1, 1–3; Esolen, 2–3.
73   *Paradiso* 10, 53; Esolen, 100–1.
74   *Paradiso* 31, 29; Esolen, 332–33.
75   "*Splendor paternae gloriae*, that is, thou, O Only-begotten, art the radiance of the Father's glory, the brightness of the most radiant glory of God the Father, of His majesty and substance, arising (*oriens*) from the fontal light of the Father.... *De luce lucem proferens*, 'O thou that bringest light from light,' that is, from thee who art the supreme light, bringing forth the Holy Spirit, who is eternal light.... Thou, O Only-begotten, art the *lux lucis*, light of light, the light that emanates from the Father, who is light not proceeding from another.... [And thou art] the *fons luminis*, that is, the fount of the Holy Spirit, who proceeds from the Father and the Son as from one fount." Blessed Denys the Carthusian, *Expositio hymni: Splendor paternae gloriae*; DCOO 35.115A–116A.

Father, breathes forth the Holy Spirit as their bond of love and the unity of their light. The whole Trinity is one essential light, and a single source of light for creatures: through His Word, and in the Holy Spirit, the Father causes the formal luminosity of things and brightens the minds of His intellectual creatures. Later in the *Paradiso* Dante says:

> All that which dies and all that dieth not
>> is naught but the splendor of the Idea
>> that the loving Father has begotten by His love.
>
> For that living Light, which so streams
>> from His shining Source, yet parts not thence,
>> nor from the Love [the Spirit] that with Them makes Three,
>
> Doth, of its goodness, gather up its rays,
>> as if mirrored, in nine subsistences,
>> eternally remaining One.[76]

Intellectual light streams from the consubstantial Word-Idea, in whom the Father knows Himself most perfectly, upon the hierarchies of the angels, and then within those hierarchies the higher angels enlighten those below them with a share in the light they have received.[77] According to St Thomas, the enlightenment of the lower angels by the higher means "manifesting the truth," that is, making the truth more accessible to them.[78]

> The idea is this [explains Abbot Vonier]: the highest spirit is through the very height of his nature endowed with vastly more knowledge than the lower spirit. Now the higher spirit gives of his superabundance to the lower spirit, and through that office of his makes the lower spirit the participant of his own excellences, and thus lifts him above his own nature, so that a spirit benefits in some degree by the excellences of all the spirits that are above him. It is thus that created causality,

---

76 *Paradiso* 13, 52–66; Sayers-Reynolds, 170.
77 For the thinking of Denys the Areopagite, on whom St Thomas depends, see ch. 1, 41–42.
78 *ST* 1a q. 106, a. 1.

which is the highest gift of the Creator to the creature, finds scope in the spirit world.[79]

Now, as human teachers discover by experience, you make the truth accessible to your pupil not just by stating it but by tracing it back to the principles from which it comes. This is how angel enlightens angel. The knowledge of the higher angels is more universal; they get the big picture.[80] Their greater minds take the broader ideas and break them up to fit them into the narrower intelligences dependent on them, just as mothers liquidize food for their infants so they can more easily swallow and digest it.[81]

All the holy angels enjoy the immediate, face-to-face vision of God, and so, on this subject, the most glorious of all, there is no need for the higher spirits to teach the lower. As the prophet says, "They shall teach no more every man his neighbor, and every man his brother, saying, 'Know the Lord,' for all shall know me, from the least of them even to the greatest" (Jer 31:34).[82] However, since there are degrees in the angels' face-to-face knowledge of God, there are also degrees in what the angels know of creatures in knowing the Creator so perfectly. The higher have much to impart to the lower concerning the meaning of the works of God, the ideas in His mind, and His application of those ideas outside Himself.[83] "The higher angel therefore knows in God secrets of the world and of history that the lower angel cannot know, or at least know in as explicit a

---

79 Vonier, *Collected Works*, 173.
80 *ST* 1a q. 55, a. 3; q. 106, a. 4, ad 1.
81 "The higher angel somehow divides up the truth that he grasps in a universal way, so that it can be taken in by the lower angel; this is how the higher angel presents the truth to the lower. Likewise, our human teachers, making provision for the capacities of other people, divide up in many different ways what they grasp in totality" (*ST* 1a q. 106, a. 1).
82 *ST* 1a q. 106, a. 1, ad 1.
83 Cf. *ST* 1a q. 106, a. 1, ad 1. "The higher angels illuminate the lower about everything known to them pertaining to the state of nature, the state of grace, and accidental glory, for the good essentially pours itself out." Reginald Garrigou-Lagrange, OP, *Commentarius in* Summam theologicam *S. Thomae*, 1a q. 27–q. 119 (Turin: Marietti, 1951), 373.

way. It is this higher knowledge of the divine mysteries that the illuminating angel communicates to the illuminated angel."[84] In seeing the Creator, the angels see in Him the universe He created in its entire development, and especially the drama of salvation history from the garden of Eden, the scene of the Fall, to the valley of Jehoshaphat, the setting of the Last Judgement. The illuminating angel, so to speak, translates his knowledge of the divine mysteries into species, ideas, that the illuminated angel can assimilate.[85] The higher angels see more clearly the "fittingness" (*convenientia*) of everything God does, that is, how what He does in creating man and the universe fits together, as a beautiful whole, with what He does in recreating man and making all things new in Christ.[86]

The more profoundly agents share in the divine goodness, the more they strive to pour their perfections into others: "As every man hath received grace, ministering the same one to another, as good stewards of the manifold grace of God" (1 Pt 4:10). After all, *bonum est diffusivum sui*: goodness tends to bubble over.[87] But the higher angels share most fully in the divine goodness. Therefore, they impart to the ones subject to them what they themselves receive from God. But what the lower angels receive from the higher angels they do not possess to the same degree of excellence. Therefore, the higher angels always remain in their higher place and have a more perfect knowledge, just as a teacher understands the same thing as his pupil, but he understands it more fully than the pupil does.[88]

---

84 Bonino, 247f.

85 Ibid., 248n, citing John of St Thomas, *Cursus theologicus* disp. 45, a. 2; t. 4, p. 834, n. 23.

86 Cf. Gilbert Narcisse, OP, *Les raisons de Dieu: Arguments et convenance et ésthetique selon St Thomas d'Aquin et Hans Urs von Balthasar* (Paris: Editions universitaires, 1997).

87 "Of its nature the good communicates itself to others" (*ST* 1a q. 106, a. 4).

88 *ST* 1a q. 106, a. 4. Yet among men it is possible for the pupil eventually to surpass the master in understanding; whereas no lower angel will surpass a higher one in this regard.

KNOWLEDGE OF SUPERNATURAL MYSTERIES

What the angels know of supernaturally revealed truth, they know only because God, by a gratuitous gift made in addition to the ideas He gave them with their nature, has disclosed these sublime secrets to them.[89] In their first state, before their testing, the angels had sanctifying grace and the infused virtue of faith, by which they gave their assent to the mysteries revealed to them by God, and in which they contemplated the mysteries.[90] But, says St Thomas, this contemplation-in-faith of the untested angels was of a higher order than the one we fallen sons of Adam have. They did not seek God, as we now seek Him, as if He were somehow absent, "since by the light of wisdom He was more present to them than He is to us, though He was not so present to them as He is to the blessed by the light of glory."[91] Now, of course, the holy angels are themselves blessed, and know the mysteries of grace most perfectly through the face-to-face vision of God. However, they do not know all the mysteries, nor do all the angels know the mysteries to the same degree.

> The higher angels, beholding the divine wisdom more clearly, know in the vision of God more and deeper mysteries, which they make manifest to the lower angels by illumination. Some of these mysteries the angels have known from the beginning of their creation; others they have learnt afterwards, according to the requirements of the offices they perform.[92]

KNOWLEDGE OF THE INCARNATION

When and how did the angels acquire their knowledge of the Incarnation? The holy angels are servants of the Word incarnate and the souls He came to save. "Are they not all ministering spirits sent forth to serve, for the sake of those who are to obtain salvation?" (Heb 1:14). Therefore, for the sake of their salvific

---

89 Cf. *ST* 1a q. 57, a. 5.
90 *ST* 2a2ae q. 5, a. 1.
91 *ST* 2a2ae q. 5, a. 1, ad 1.
92 *ST* 1a q. 57, a. 5.

mission, it was revealed to all the holy angels, from the beginning of their heavenly beatitude, that the Son of God would become incarnate of the Virgin Mary for us men and our salvation. The Incarnation, says St Thomas, "is a kind of general principle governing all the offices" of the angels.[93] The Master of the *Sentences*, Peter Lombard, had claimed that "the higher angels had long known of the mystery of the Incarnation, whereas the lower angels did not know until it had taken place." In his reply, St Thomas interprets the Master to mean not that "the lower angels from the beginning were entirely ignorant of the mystery of the Incarnation, but rather that their knowledge of it was not as good as that of higher angels, and so, when it did take place, they advanced in their knowledge of it."[94] As the Son of God ascends into Heaven in the substance of our human flesh, the lower angels cry out in wonder, "Who is this King of Glory?" And the angels of higher rank respond, enlightening them: "The Lord of the heavenly powers" (cf. Ps 23:18).[95]

St Paul seems to imply that the angels, "the Principalities and Powers," learnt of the mystery of salvation in Christ through the preaching of the Church (cf. Eph 3:10). St Peter likewise says that "angels long to look into" what has been revealed (cf. 1 Pt 1:12). St Jerome concludes that the angels heard of the Incarnation through the preaching of the Apostles.[96] But Blessed Denys the Areopagite, referring to the Gospels, is adamant that the angels knew of the Incarnation before men did:

> I note that the mystery of Jesus' love for mankind was first revealed to the angels, and then the grace of this knowledge was granted by the angels to us. It was the most divine Gabriel who instructed Zachariah the hierarch in the mystery that, contrary to all hope and by God's grace, he would have a child who would be a prophet of the human-divine work of Jesus, who in

93 *ST* 1a q. 57, a. 5, ad 1.
94 *ST* 1a q. 106, a. 4, ad 2.
95 Cf. Dionysius the Areopagite, *De caelesti hierarchia*, cap. 7, n. 3; OG 3.09AB.
96 Cf. St Jerome, *Commentarii in epistolam ad Ephesios* 2; PL 26.514C–515B.

his loving kindness was about to appear for the salvation of the world. Gabriel revealed to Mary how in her would be accomplished the divine mystery of the ineffable conception of God. Another angel tells Joseph how the divine promises made to his ancestor David would in truth be fulfilled. Yet another angel brought the good news to the shepherds, who in silence and withdrawal from the world had been purified. And with him "a multitude of the heavenly host" handed on to those on earth the doxology of high renown.[97]

In any case, argues St Thomas, just as the lower angels are enlightened by the higher, but do not enlighten them, so men cannot enlighten even the lowest of the angels. St John the Baptist is the greatest of all the men born of women, but the least of the angels in the Kingdom of Heaven is greater than he (cf. Mt 11:11).[98] Therefore, the angels cannot have learnt of the Incarnation through the preaching of the Apostles, who are lower than the Baptist in the hierarchy of holiness. The texts in the epistles of Saints Peter and Paul mentioned above, says St Thomas, following St Augustine, imply not that the angels were altogether ignorant of the mystery of Christ and the Church before the Apostles started proclaiming it, but that "certain things became apparent to the angels that before had been hidden from them": for example, that the Gentiles would be converted through the preaching of St Paul.[99]

FIRM, FULL, AND FREE: THE ANGELIC WILL

The world of God's creation moves in a rhythm of departure and return. Everything comes from His will, as an overflow of His love for His Supreme Goodness, and so everything loves the Good and longs to go back to It, *to Him*. But each kind of thing loves and longs for the good in its own way. Inanimate bodies and plants move towards the good, their goal,

97 Dionysius the Areopagite, *De caelesti hierarchia*, cap. 4, n. 4; PG 3.1813E.
98 Cf. *ST* 1a q. 117, a. 2.
99 Cf. *ST* 1a q. 117, a. 2, ad 1.

without any knowledge, by a "natural appetite." With admirable persistence and sublime unawareness, Old Father Thames rolls along down to the mighty sea, and the anemone lifts her head to the sun. Animals are inclined to the good by "sense appetite," with knowledge through their senses of a particular good, but with no idea of goodness as such: the mouse knows this yellow stuff is good to eat, but he can't tell you what "good" means. Best of all are those inclined to the good with intellectual knowledge of what the good is. This inclination is the will, the "intellectual appetite," the desire of creatures blessed with intellect, such as the angels.[100] The angels are created in the image of the Blessed Trinity, as human beings are. Now within the Godhead the Father begets the Son by way of intellect as Word, and the Father and the Son breathe forth the Holy Spirit by way of will as Love. In both men and angels, therefore, but more perfectly in the angels, there is will, the capacity to love, as well as intellect.

The will of the angels is free; they can choose one thing rather than another. Old Father Thames cannot do anything except roll along down to the sea. The mouse seems to be choosing a smart course of action when he runs away from the cat, but he acts by unthinking instinct; escape is Jerry's only option. But creatures with intellect have knowledge of goodness in general, and so can judge this or that particular thing to be good. Where there is intellect, there is freedom. Such is the judgement, such the will, of the intellectual substances we call the angels.[101] Angelic action is free, not forced.

The free will of the angel is more perfect than that of man. Unlike human beings, the bodiless spirit makes his choices without inquiry or deliberation; he simply sees the true and goes for the good.[102] As a purely spiritual and intellectual creature, the angel has no senses or sense appetites; and so his will cannot be blocked or diverted by the passions of the appetites. Now when

---

100 Cf. *ST* 1a q. 59, a. 1.
101 Cf. *ST* 1a q. 59, a. 3.
102 Cf. *ST* 1a q. 59, a. 3, ad 1.

something does not block nature, or hold it back, nature moves forward with all the majesty of its God-given power. Therefore, when the angels make a free decision, there are no hesitations or half-measures; they exercise their free will with a vigor and totality of commitment undreamt of by men.[103] Once angels start choosing, it is all or nothing.

Angels have will and can therefore love. Like human beings, they have a natural appetite for their own final good, their happiness and fulfilment; by the necessity of nature, each loves himself.[104] But angels also love freely; their wills are fixed to the good as such, but not to this or that good. They have an elective will.[105] They love particular goods somehow related to their fulfilment, and so, by the choosing of those goods, too, they love themselves.[106] But by the necessity of nature, like men, the angels love God more than they love themselves. When something belongs to something else, it is more inclined to that other thing than to itself: for example, my hand instinctively wards off a blow that would hurt the body as a whole, even if the hand itself is hurt. Moreover, since reason imitates nature, we find a similar service of the whole by the part in the rational acts of the good citizen: he is ready to lay down his life for his country.[107] Now, since every creature, angel and man, belongs to God, the universal Good and source of all goodness, it follows that angels and men by an instinctive natural love, first and foremost and above all, love God more than themselves. Every desire that the God of infinite wisdom and goodness implants in the nature of His intellectual creatures, angels or men, is true and upright, even if in men, as a consequence of original sin and their personal sins, the desire is weakened and diminished. Charity, the love of God above all else, infused into the wills of angels and men by the Holy Spirit, presupposes, as it also

---

103   Cf. *ST* 1a q. 62, a. 6.
104   Cf. *ST* 1a q. 60, a. 3.
105   Cf. *ST* 1a q. 60, a. 2).
106   "Angel and man naturally seek their own good and perfection; that is, each loves himself" (*ST* 1a q. 60, a. 3).
107   Cf. *ST* 1a q. 60, a. 5.

perfects and does not destroy, this natural inclination to love God, the sovereign good, more than themselves.[108]

→←

THE DEMONS FELL THROUGH PRIDE AND THE choosing of their own good in contempt of God. The holy angels were humble and modest, and now, as Beatrice helps Dante to understand, their glorified wills partake of God's own freedom. The hierarchs of heaven are now so much at liberty that they are free from the possibility of sinning.

> But these kept humble tenor, know themselves
>   as rising from the generosity
>   that made them quick to understand so much.
>
> So were their eyes exalted, raised thus high
>   By merit and illuminating grace
>   and now their will is firm and full and free.[109]

---

108   Cf. *ST* 1a q. 60, a. 5; Reginald Garrigou-Lagrange, *De Deo trino et creatore: Commentarius in* Summam theologicam S. *Thomae* (1a qq. 27–119) (Turin: Marietti, 1951), 364–66.
109   *Paradiso* 29, 58–63; Esolen, 312–13.

BOTTICELLI, PARADISO 30

3

GUARDING THE · VALE

WHAT THE GOOD ANGELS DO

G OD, THE BLESSED TRINITY, GOVERNS the material universe through a multitude of angels and guards the individual human being by the ministry of an angel specially created by Him for the purpose. Governing and guarding, however, are not the principal tasks of the angels, as Dante indicates when he describes the second of the three angelic hierarchies.

> The second triad which is flowering yet
>   In this eternal, never-fading Spring,
>   Ne'er by the Ram in his night-raids beset,
>
> With its perpetual Hosanna-ing
>   Sings winter out in triple melody,
>   In threefold bliss within its treble ring.[1]

Just as the birds burst into song in earthly spring, so the angels "sing winter out" in the "eternal, never-fading Spring" of Paradise, in a perpetual praise of God that never falters in its joy.

> During winter [says Louis Bouyer], how could we possibly believe, or even imagine, unless we had previously experienced it, that the world would once again be what it does become every Spring? Christians can live in the expectation of the eternal Spring that is to come. Only then shall we discover the world as it is in its deepest reality, as it will last forever. It is the world as the angels

---

1   *Paradiso* 28, 115–120; Sayers-Reynolds, 304.

have always known it, and as God's elect, who have
reached perfection, are beginning to discover... and
as we are called to discover in our turn.[2]

Working only with charcoal on paper, Botticelli attempts an
image of the undying Spring of the blessed. In his illustration of
Canto 30, he shows us Beatrice leading Dante beside a river of
light, "golden with brightness," its banks "painted with wonderful Spring."[3] Beatrice, "the sunlight of [his] eyes," points as ever
upward. We learn from the text that the poet has to soak his
eyes in the river's liquid luminosity, in order to see the truth of
which the river and "the laughter of the flowers" are but a promise: "the shining white rose" of "the holy militia that Christ made
his Bride by his Blood."[4] Into the petals of this great bloom of
sanctity, which Botticelli does not attempt to represent, fly the
holy angels, like bees dipping for nectar, and from it they reascend,
all the while "seeing and singing the glory of Him who moves
them to love, the goodness that makes them what they are."[5]
This is "unwintering" worship, the seeing and glorifying of the
one true God, the Most Holy Trinity, in the unending season of
new life. It is the principal task of the angels. With the ancients
and the four living creatures, the holy angels bow down before
God's throne, and adore Him: "Amen. Benediction and glory and
wisdom and thanksgiving, honor and power and strength, to our
God forever and ever" (Apoc 7:12). The holy angels who serve
God in the running of the universe and the protecting of the sons
of Adam are first of all beholders and worshipers of the Triune
God, and of the Lamb of God (cf. Apoc 5:12). Their presence
and activity on earth and among the stars makes the cosmos
liturgical of its very nature and in all its parts. "The heavens show
forth the glory of God, and the firmament declareth the work
of His hands" (Ps 18:2).

---

2   Louis Bouyer, *Cosmos: Le monde et la gloire de Dieu* (Paris: Cerf, 1982),
204f.
3   *Paradiso* 30, 61–62; author's translation.
4   *Paradiso* 31, 1–3; author's translation.
5   *Paradiso* 31, 5–6; author's translation.

ASSISTING AND MINISTERING:
ANGELS IN HEAVEN AND ON EARTH

God sends some angels to do something for Him on earth: "Behold I will send my angel who shall go before thee" (Ex 23:20). According to Blessed Denys and St Gregory, the higher ranks "do not have any external ministry,"[6] but simply and ceaselessly cry "Holy, holy, holy" to the Lord God of Hosts (cf. Is 6:7). Heaven is their home and the all-absorbing interest of their existence; they are "the domestics of God, the citizens of heaven, and the princes of Paradise."[7] But in addition to the angels that *assist* in heaven, there are others that *administer* on earth, just as in a kingdom there are the king's courtiers, always on hand in his presence, and the king's good servants administering his departments and provinces.[8] All the angels, however, even those dispatched on a ministry, continue to assist at God's throne in the sense of enjoying the direct vision of the Godhead.

> All the angels see the Divine Essence immediately. In this sense, all, even those who minister, are said to assist. Hence Gregory says that "those sent on an external ministry for our salvation can always assist and see the face of the Father." Yet not all the angels can perceive the secrets of the divine mysteries in the clarity of the Divine Essence itself; only the higher angels, who announce the mysteries to the lower, have such clear perception, and in this sense only the higher angels belonging to the first hierarchy are said to assist. It is proper to them, says Denys, to be enlightened immediately by God.[9]

Those who most properly assist are the ones who most perfectly see. They transmit the light in which they see Light to those angels below them, who also see but with less perspicuity.[10]

6　Cited by St Thomas in the *sed contra* of *ST* 1a q. 112, a. 2.
7　St Bernard of Clairvaux, *In festo S. Michaelis, sermo* 1, n. 1; PL 183.447D.
8　Cf. *ST* 1a q. 112, a. 3.
9　*ST* 1a q. 112, a. 3.
10　At the end of the world, says our Lord, "the angels will go out, and will separate the wicked from among the just" (Mt 13:49). In saying the angels

The inspiration and permanent accompaniment of the angels' ministry on earth and throughout the visible universe is their contemplation of God in heaven. The archangel Gabriel, sent to announce the conception and birth of St John the Baptist, tells Zechariah the priest that he "stands in the presence of God" (cf. Lk 1:19). Commenting on our Lord's words to Nathanael, "You shall see heaven opened and the angels of God ascending and descending upon the Son of Man" (Jn 1:51), St Bernard says: "The blessed spirits ascend through contemplation of God, and descend out of compassion for you, that they may guard you in all your ways. They ascend to His countenance, and descend at His command, for He has given His angels charge over you. But in descending they are not robbed of the vision of His glory, for they always behold the face of the Father."[11] What comes first in the life of the celestial hierarchy is what should come first in the life of the ecclesiastical hierarchy: the worship of God the Most High, the Holy and Undivided Trinity.

"THE PERFECT CONGRUENCE":
ANGELS AND THE VISIBLE UNIVERSE

> ... wondrous is the perfect congruence
>   Which every heaven with every mover shows
>   Between their corresponding movements.[12]

In ancient and medieval cosmology, the planets, with the sun and the moon, circle the earth in a series of concentric globes: the "celestial spheres" of the moon, Mercury, Venus, the sun, Mars, Jupiter, and Saturn. Beyond these seven are the sphere of the fixed stars and then the *primum mobile*, the first movable body, which imparts motion to the other eight spheres. Transcending the nine spheres is the Empyrean, the fiery heaven,

---

"go out," He does not mean "they depart from the intimacy of contemplation, because, wherever they are, they contemplate God." Our Lord's point is that they go forth to an exterior ministry while remaining beholders of the face of the Father (cf. St Thomas, *Super Matthaeum*, cap. 13, lect. 4).
11   St Bernard of Clairvaux, *Sermo* 11, n. 6; PL 183.227AB.
12   *Paradiso* 28, 76–78; Sayers-Reynolds, 303.

which is the dwelling-place of God. Now, according to Dante, in the service of God's Providence each heaven is under the management of an angelic order: the Seraphim move the *Primum mobile*, the Cherubim the heaven of the fixed stars, and the other seven orders, from the Thrones to the plain and simple Angels, guide the seven planetary spheres from Saturn to the Moon.[13] The chart of the cosmos used by Dante is the one he and his contemporaries inherited from Ptolemy and the ancients, with the earth at the center. We now know that the earth is part of the "solar system," the cluster of planets that circle the sun, and that the sun is one of a myriad of stars in a galaxy in a universe of a myriad of galaxies. However, despite the obsolescence of the astrophysics, the philosophical and theological principles underlying Dante's vision, principles he received from the Church's Fathers and Doctors, remain permanently valid. Ignoring them will impoverish our understanding of the mysteries of God's creation.

As we have seen, in the plan of God's Providence, both the visible universe of bodily things and the invisible world of the angels have the structure of a *hierarchy*, what a Welsh Catholic poet has called "graded plurality."[14] Lower things are governed by higher things: rule and communication on the one hand; dependence and receptivity on the other. The pattern of dependence within a hierarchy can be seen most easily in material things. For example, the functioning of humble limbs and organs is under the control of the great organ of the brain; and without the sun's light and heat, the earth would be a lump of frozen

---

13   "Are the heavenly bodies endowed with a soul, or are they simply moved externally? The medievals debated the question. According to St Thomas, the heavenly bodies belong to a region of the universe of an utterly different kind to our sublunary world, and they cannot therefore be moved by nature. Without rejecting absolutely the thesis of an animation of Heaven, St Thomas holds that the celestial body is moved by an extrinsic power of intellectual nature, which is an angel belonging to the second Dionysian hierarchy, the Virtues." Bonino, 68n217; cf. *ST* 1a q. 70, a. 3.
14   Saunders Lewis, "The Essence of Welsh Poetry," in Harri Pritchard Jones, *Saunders Lewis: A Presentation of His Work* (Springfield, Illinois: Templegate, 1990), 103.

rock. Egalitarian uniformity in creatures is the mark of disorder, as is evident in the pointless multiplication of cancer cells. Now, according to St Thomas, not only are lesser material things governed by greater things, the whole of the material order, ever in flux, is moved and directed, under God, by the relatively immobile spiritual substances that Catholic Tradition calls the angels, who themselves are ordered in a celestial hierarchy. In God's wisdom and love, the whole corporeal universe and the entire history of mankind, with all its members, are under the mighty and courteous care of God's holy angels. Pure spirits though they are, the holy angels have a connection with the world of bodies.[15] Unlike the fallen angels, they are not hostile to matter and the flesh.

In arguing for the part played by the angels under God in His governing of bodily creatures, St Thomas quotes two Patristic authorities: "All bodies are ruled by a rational spirit of life" (St Augustine in the *De Trinitate*); "In this visible world nothing takes place without the agency of the invisible creature" (St Gregory the Great in the *Dialogues*). In the third article of the same question, Thomas, who here follows Denys, says: "Lower nature at its highest point is touched by higher nature."

> It is a favorite theme with St Thomas Aquinas [says Abbot Vonier] to represent the whole physical world

---

[15] "God governs lower creatures both through spiritual creatures and through the more noble bodily creatures, but in different ways. His Providence works through bodily creatures by making them not provident, but only agents. Through spiritual creatures His Providence works by making them provident" (*De veritate* q. 5, a. 8). Preaching in Oxford, the young Newman expounds the same doctrine as the Fathers cited by St Thomas. As he looks out at the silver of the morning mist over Christ Church Meadow or sees the golden glow of college stone in the setting sun, his mind's eye glimpses the blessed spirits, who, under God their Creator, sustain this beautiful earth: "Whenever we look abroad, we are reminded of those most gracious and holy beings, the servants of the Holiest, who deign to minister to the heirs of salvation. Every breath of air and ray of light and heat, every beautiful prospect, is, as it were, the skirts of their garments, the waving of the robes whose faces see God in heaven" (John Henry Newman, "The Powers of Nature," *Parochial and Plain Sermons*, vol. 2, 362).

as being entrusted by God to the keeping of the angels. The stars in their courses are watched by the mighty spirits; nations are committed to the care of a heavenly prince; and there is no part of the universe which does not feel the breath of those whose mind beholds the countenance of God. An all-pervading principle governs the theology of the spirit ministry — namely, an inferior thing in creation is invariably under the tutelage of a higher thing. To this great law there is no exception. The universe is held together with the golden threads of spirit power as well as with the coarser sinews of natural energy.[16]

In the first article of question 110 in the First Part of the *Summa,* St Thomas tells us that the ruling of the material world by the bodiless spirits, for which he argues from the authority of the Fathers, is also the teaching of the philosophers.[17] As we have seen, Plato made the claim that immaterial substances were "the essences and species of sensible bodies," and had "direct supervision (*praesidentiam*) over all sensible bodies."[18] Aristotle argued, by contrast, that immaterial substances are not the species of sensible bodies, but "something higher and more universal"; however, these superior spiritual substances presided over the heavenly bodies with their wide and universal agency, not over particular things.[19] Here is a point on which Aquinas differs from

16   Vonier, *Teaching,* 268. "Nature is not inanimate; its daily toil is intelligent; its works are *duties*. Accordingly, the Psalmist says, 'The heavens declare the glory of God, and the firmament showeth His handy-work'. . . . I do not pretend to say that we are told in Scripture what matter is; but I affirm, that as our souls move our bodies, be our bodies what they may, so there are Spiritual Intelligences which move those wonderful and vast portions of the natural world which seem to be inanimate; and as the gestures, speech, and expressive countenances of our friends around us enable us to hold intercourse with them, so in the motions of universal Nature, in the interchange of day and night, summer and winter, wind and storm, fulfilling His word, we are reminded of the blessed and dutiful Angels" (John Henry Newman, "The Powers of Nature," 361).
17   Cf. *ST* 1a q. 110, a. 1.
18   On the angelology of the philosophers, see 23ff.
19   *ST* 1a, q. 110, a. 1, ad 3.

Aristotle: angels, in Aquinas's opinion, *do* have a direct control over lower bodies.[20]

The angels are superior to bodily creatures not only in what they are, but also in what they can do, even to bodily creatures. As we learn from Scripture, angels can move material things from one place to another: for example, an angel stirs up the water of the pool of Bethsaida (cf. Jn 5:4), and another rolls back the stone from the tomb of Jesus (cf. Mt 28:2). Moreover, says St Thomas, "by first causing a change of place, angels can cause other changes, that is, by using bodily agencies to produce these effects, as a blacksmith uses fire to melt iron."[21] As naturally embodied creatures, we assume that the lack of hands and arms and legs is a disadvantage to pure spirits when they start moving material objects around. The opposite is true: "The motive power of the soul [says St Thomas] is limited to the body united to it, which is vivified by it, and by which it can move other things. But an angel's power is not limited to a body; hence it can cause local movement in bodies not joined to it."[22] There are limits on the number of balls that even a juggler can keep in the air. An angel is not so constrained. Of the angel-boatman who ferries the holy souls to purgatory, Dante's Virgil says:

> See how he holds man's instruments in scorn:
>   he needs no oars nor any other sail
>   but his own wings toward such distant shores.[23]

But does the cosmic stewardship of the angels not make the laws of physics redundant? What room is there for molecules and sub-atomic particles in a material world administered by angels? Abbot Vonier supplies the answer:

> The theological theory of the universe leaves the physical theory completely untouched. It supposes merely that the wise Creator, who governs the material universe in

20 *ST* 1a, q. 110, a. 1, ad 2.
21 Cf. *ST* 1a q. 110, a. 3, ad 1.
22 Cf. *ST* 1a q. 110, a. 3, ad 3.
23 *Purgatorio* 2, 31–33; Esolen, 14–15.

accordance with the uniform laws of nature that He has made, makes use, in the application of those laws, of angels as intermediaries and executors of His plan. Nor ought we to consider those created activities of the spirits superfluous on account of God's omnipresent vigilance over His universe. God multiplies created power, not because He could not effect the result Himself, but because it is a more beautiful universe which has a hierarchy of potentialities.[24]

This last sentence of the abbot is of immense importance. Failure to grasp it can lead to serious doctrinal error. According to the wisdom of the Church, God is at work in the actions of His creatures. *He causes His creatures, including the angels, to cause.* The First Cause works in and through the works of secondary causes.[25] Whatever is a reality outside of God, including the acts of the free will of men and angels,[26] is caused by divine motion. No creature is self-sufficient in either being or activity. This is the teaching of the Prophet Isaiah and the Apostle Paul as well as a conclusion that can be reached through an argument of natural reason: "Lord, thou hast wrought all our works in us" (Is 26:12). "It is God who worketh in you, both to will and to accomplish, according to His good will" (Phil 2:13).

God's causality, whether in the natural order or in the supernatural, does not overwhelm or replace creaturely causality; rather the First Cause produces and guarantees the effectiveness of secondary causes. "God's acting in creatures ... must be understood in such a way that they themselves still exercise

---

24 Vonier, *Teaching*, 268f.

25 "Where there are several agents arranged in order, the second always acts in virtue of the first; for the first agent moves the second to act. In this way, all agents act in virtue of God Himself; and therefore He is the cause of action in every agent" (St Thomas, *ST* 1a q. 105, a. 5). "God is at work in all secondary causes, and all their effects are traced back to God as to a cause" (*SCG* lib. 3, cap. 75, n. 5).

26 "To move freely is to move of oneself, that is, from an intrinsic principle; but this intrinsic principle can be from an extrinsic principle; and so to move oneself does not exclude being moved by another" (St Thomas, *ST* 1a q. 105, a. 4, ad 2).

their own operations."[27] He moves His creatures to act in such a way that the act is truly their own. The capacity to cause is His wise and loving gift to them: "God governs lower things through higher, not because of a defect in His power, but because, in the abundance of His goodness, He communicates the dignity of causality to creatures."[28] Blessed Denys the Carthusian expands St Thomas's argument:

> God is by nature good and by essence charity itself. Therefore, though He could by Himself alone without difficulty rule the universe and move and produce all He produces and moves through secondary causes, nevertheless, for the full declaration of His goodness and charity, He communicated to creatures, especially intellectual ones, causal, providential, and governing power.[29]

Abbot Vonier explains the doctrine of the Angelic and Ecstatic Doctors with his customary clarity:

> The Catholic view...is that the greatest and highest communication of God is the participation of causality. Not only is He the cause of all things and all good, but He makes His creatures also to be, in their respective degree, causes of things and causes of good; and in our metaphysics, as well as in our piety, we go by this principle, that the highest creature is also the most powerful creature, and that the more God loves a spiritual being, the more means He gives to that being of doing good to others.[30]

That is why the Mother of God, more glorious than the Seraphim, is the Mediatrix of All Graces, blessing and enriching the life of

---

27 St Thomas, *ST* 1a q. 105, a. 5. "God works in every natural thing, not as though the natural thing did not work at all, but because God works in both nature and will when they work" (St Thomas, *De potentia* q. 3, a. 7).
28 *ST* 1a q. 22, a. 3. God makes use of intermediate causes "so that the beauty of order be preserved, and that He may communicate to creatures the dignity of causality" (*ST* 1a q. 23, a. 8, ad 2).
29 Denys the Carthusian, *Elementatio theologica*, prop. 72; DCOO 33.171AB.
30 Vonier, *Collected Works*, 168.

every man who does not resist the gentle action of the Holy Spirit of her Son. That, too, is why created spirits do so much good in the lives of individual human beings, in the general history of mankind, and in the entire cosmos. Their powerful causality is dependent upon the omnipotence, wisdom, and love of God, and manifests the perfection of Divine Providence.[31]

The governing and guarding work of the angels, like the secondary causality of all creatures, is first of all God's work; it is truly theirs, but only because it is first of all His. So we must not think that the almighty Creator leaves the running of the universe to the angels without being interested or involved, like an absentee landlord. God's wise and loving Providence operates in and through the operation of His holy angels. God Himself moves bodily creatures into action with the cooperation of His purely spiritual creatures. As Fr Bonino says:

---

31   The *sinfulness* of human and demonic acts is not, of course, something that comes from God. Sin is not some*thing*, not a positively existing substance, but a privation, a wound, the disorder in our conduct. This destructive negativity comes from nowhere but the defective causality of our unruly wills. Of my sins I must confess what the pavement artist claims, "All my own work." By contrast, every good action, whether natural or supernatural, has its first mover in God, who, as the Roman Catechism says, "by means of an internal power, impels to motion and action everything that moves and acts, and this in such a manner that, although He excludes not, He yet precedes the agency of secondary causes" (*Catechism of the Council of Trent for Parish Priests*, ed. and trans. John A. McHugh, OP, & Charles J. Callan, OP [New York: Wagner, 1947], 30). "The act of sin is both a being and an act; and in both respects it is from God, for every being, whatever the mode of its being, must be derived from the First Being, as Denys makes clear. Every action is caused by something that actually exists, since nothing acts unless it actually exists. Now everything that actually exists is derived from the First Act, namely God, as to its cause, who is act by His essence. Therefore, God is the cause of every action, insofar as it is an action. But sin denotes a being and an action with some defect, and this defect is from the created cause, namely, free will, defecting from the order of the First Agent, namely, God. So this defect cannot be traced back to God as its cause, but to free will. The defect of limping can be traced back to the crooked leg as its cause, but it cannot be traced back to the motive power, which nevertheless causes whatever movement there is in the limping. In this way, then, God is the cause of the *act* of sin: and yet He is *not the cause of sin*, because He does not cause the act to have a defect" (St Thomas, *ST* 1a2ae q. 79, a. 2).

True, bodily beings have actions determined by their nature, but to exercise them, to pass over to act, they need to be moved by a spiritual reality that activates them.... No being can make itself pass from potency to act. This actualization has its source in God, First Act, but nothing prevents us from thinking that this "physical pre-motion" is transmitted by the habitual action of angels.... The physical universe — and still more the psychological universe — are "open" universes, leaving room for initiatives depending on the "creativity" of certain autonomous centers of finalized free acting.[32]

Pascal confessed he was frightened by the "silence of these infinite spaces."[33] But there are no grounds for fear. The stars, and all other bodily things in the universe, are created and moved by the God who is love, and are placed by Him under the sweet influence of the holy angels. "Denys says that divine love moves higher things to the providential care of lower things."[34] Man need not be afraid, because even in the remotest places of the universe he has God-given friends. The empty spaces of the galaxies are not silent, for they resound with the chanting of the angels in praise of the Blessed Trinity: *Sanctus, sanctus, sanctus Dominus Deus Sabaoth.*

"WATCHFUL CARE": ANGELS AS GUARDIANS

One of the poor souls in Dante's Purgatory, Sordello the troubadour, speaks of the guarding mission of the angels.

"They come from Mary's heart," said Sordello,
    "to guard the vale; for very soon
    the Serpent comes."[35]

Catholics hold by faith that God has deputed certain of the holy angels to guard human beings on their journey through this

---

32 Bonino, 83, 84.
33 Pascal, *Pensées* n. 206 (London & Paris: Dent & Crés, 1913), 94.
34 *Sent.* lib. 3, d. 32, q. 1, a. 2, *sed contra* 2.
35 *Purgatorio* 8, 37–39; Sayers, 127.

vale of tears to their true native land in heaven. "From infancy to death," says the *Catechism of the Catholic Church*, "human life is surrounded by their watchful care and intercession."[36] Each of us has at his side a protector deputed by God, "a soldier," says St Hildegard, "of celestial harmony, light-filled and pure, abiding in the vision of God."[37] He wields a sword of immaterial fire to drive away the attacks of the enemy and reinforce the holy armor of God. This is the teaching of Jesus himself: "See that you despise not one of these little ones; for I say to you that their angels in heaven always see the face of my Father who is in heaven" (Mt 18:10). David, in one of the Psalms, sees the destiny of every man enveloped within angelic intelligence and love: "He hath given His angels charge over thee, to keep thee in all thy ways" (Ps 90:11). The devoted service of men, lowly flesh and blood, by the bodiless powers of heaven should astonish but also console us: "In the spirits above [writes St Bernard] we find not only a wonderful dignity, but also a most lovable condescension."[38]

Speaking of the angels of the little ones who believe in Christ, St Basil the Great says: "Every one of the faithful has an angel at his side as teacher and shepherd, directing his life."[39] St Jerome throws the mantle of angelic protection even wider: "Great is the dignity of souls, that each should have an angel delegated to guard it from its birth."[40] For St Gregory Nazianzen, the guardian angel is "a protector."[41] The Fathers testify from their own experience to the guardian angels' protection of souls and bodies from demonic assault. St Macarius the Great had a vision of demons attacking a young man who was visiting him, while

---

36 CCC 335.
37 St Hildegard, *Scivias* Pars 3, visio 2, cap. 19; CCCM 43A.365.
38 St Bernard of Clairvaux, *In festo S. Michaelis, sermo* 1, n. 1; PL 183.447D. "You are not alone. You are in the hands of someone who sees you and sees God, who sees the face of God and in God's light sees you." Romano Guardini, *Engel: Theologische Betrachtungen* (Mainz: Matthias-Grünewald-Verlag, 1995), 33.
39 St Basil the Great, *Adversus Eunomium* 3, 1; PG 29.656B.
40 *In evangelium Matthaei* 18, 10; PL 26.130B.
41 *Poemata de seipso* 3, 5–8; PG 37.1020A.

the holy angel circled about him "with a fiery sword chasing the demons far from him."[42] When the Desert Father Moses was afflicted by grievous temptations, his friend Abbot Isidore told him to look west, to see the demons ready for battle and hurrying to the fight, and then to turn to the east, "where he saw the innumerable multitude of the holy angels, the glorious and resplendent army of the heavenly powers, outshining the light of the sun." Abbot Isidore invites Abbot Moses to draw consolation from the vision he has been shown: "The ones you saw in the East are the ones God sends to help His holy ones. Know this, as the prophet Elisha says, there are more on our side than on the enemy's. . . . Comforted in the Lord by what he heard, the holy Abbot Moses returned to his cell, giving thanks, and glorifying the patience of the goodness of our Lord Jesus Christ."[43]

St Bernard of Clairvaux urges his monks to love the guardian angels with gratitude for what they do for us, and in hope for what we shall share with them:

> In Him, brethren, let us love His angels with affection, as coheirs with us in the future, and in the present appointed and set over us by the Father as our agents and protectors. We are now the sons of God, even though it does not it appear what we shall be; we are still little ones under protectors and agents, no different from servants. Even though we are so small, and the road that lies ahead is not only long but dangerous, what need we fear with such great guardians? Those who guard us in all our ways cannot be overcome, nor be led astray, still less lead us astray. They are faithful, they are prudent, they are powerful: what have we to fear? Let us just follow them, let us cling to them, and we shall abide in the protection of the God of heaven.[44]

The poet Claudel presents the same thought in verse:

---

42   *The Sayings of the Desert Fathers: The Alphabetic Collection*, 135.
43   *De vitis patrum*, lib. 3, *Verba seniorum* n.10; PL 73.744AB.
44   *In Psalmum 90, Qui habitat, sermo* 12, n. 7; PL 183.234BC.

No one kneels and no one prays,
No one bends to God his mind,
No one weeps his wasted days,
No one can with sobs unbind
His secret thought to Mary's Son
But feels his shrouded soul is won
And down its labyrinthine maze,
Melodiously intertwined,
The lovely choirs of angels run.
Oh, revelation of the friend!
Of our brother, heaven-assigned
To guide us if our spirit sways
And set us, when his task is done,
Among the princely ranks inclined
No more to live in married ways.
The Father opens arms to none
Who is not as a little one....
No path we march on is too steep
But that an angel van may keep.
Beside the sick, the old, may go
A spirit whom God calls His friend.[45]

What the angels do in the governing of the universe and the guarding of our individual lives, they do as the servants of the wisdom and love of His Providence. In the words of St Thomas: "The guardianship of the angels is a kind of carrying out of the Divine Providence over men."[46] The guardian angels, in Abbot Vonier's happy phrase, are in themselves "Providence in practice, and therefore they become one of the main factors in the world's course."[47] And so the Church prays on their feast day: "O God, who in thine ineffable Providence hast vouchsafed to send holy angels to guard us, grant us, who make our humble prayer to thee, ever to be defended by their protection, and to enjoy their fellowship without end."

---

45 Paul Claudel, "Hymne aux saints anges," *Oeuvre poétique* (Paris: Galli-mard, 1967), 455f. The translation is by Sister Mary David, SSND, in her Claudel collection, *Coronal* (New York: Pantheon, 1943), 169–73.
46 Cf. *ST* q. 113, a. 6.
47 Abbot Vonier, *Collected Works*, vol. 3, 166.

In the visible world, with its change and decay, man, the fallen rational creature, has a particular fragility: his knowledge and affectivity can easily deviate from the good. "Therefore [concludes St Thomas], it was necessary that angels should be deputed to guard men, so that they might be directed and moved toward the good."[48] The guardian angels, says St Bernard, "come down from heaven to console, to visit, to help."[49] But in what ways do they help us? Charles René Billuart, the eighteenth-century Dominican commentator on the *Summa*, summarizes the testimony of Scripture and Tradition as follows:

> They illuminate our minds, not by infusing ideas, but by adapting truths to our capacity, representing them under sensible likenesses. In this way they instruct and teach us, and suggest good thoughts, and arouse the will by persuading and encouraging it towards the good. They supply occasions of good and remove occasions of evil.... They offer our prayers and intentions to God.... They keep off external harm, aid us in danger, in war, and especially in death. They drive away diseases, plagues, and so on.... They ward off and coerce the demons, lest they harm us, or at least lest they harm us as much as they would wish.[50]

Of these benevolent functions, it is the illumination of our minds that is the principal and most powerful influence of our guardian angels upon us. Intellectual light flows from the highest of the angels to the lowest, and so to men. In the National Gallery in London there is a beautiful image of the angelic enlightening of man. It is a painting by Velázquez in which a guardian angel helps the Christian soul, represented as a three-year-old child, to contemplate Christ in His scourging.

But how do our guardian angels enlighten us? Angels, holy or fallen, cannot act *directly* on our intellects any more than they can move our wills. But the bodiless spirits, good and bad, can

---

48 *ST* 1a q. 113, a. 1.
49 St Bernard of Clairvaux, *In festo S. Michaelis, sermo* 1, n. 2; PL 183.449D.
50 C. R. Billuart, OP, *Cursus theologiae iuxta mentem divi Thomae*, t. 3 (Paris: Mequignon, 1827), 427f.

affect our bodies, and our senses, external and internal, especially our imagination and memory. By clothing an idea in a sensible image (a "sensible likeness," as Billuart puts it), they set our minds on a new, wholesome, and holy train of thought. We receive our knowledge through the working of the senses; and our thinking involves turning back to images, rooting the universals of our thought in the particulars of our experience. That is the way God has made us, and that is how God's servants, our guardian angels, shine the light of truth on our minds.

> The human intellect [says St Thomas] cannot grasp intelligible truth in its nakedness, since it is connatural to the human intellect to understand by turning to sense-images. Therefore, the angels propose intelligible truth to men under the likenesses of sensible things. As Denys says: "It is impossible for the divine light to shine upon us unless it be shrouded by a variety of sacred veils."[51]

What of the angels' influence on our wills? They cannot move them on the inside, by inclining them to something; only God can move the will in that way, because it is He, says St Thomas, "who endows intellectual nature with the power of such an inclination."[52] Only the Author of nature is the author of the creature's natural inclination; only He can be the first cause of the rational creature's voluntary inclination. However, angels, holy or fallen, working outside the human will, can change it by persuasion, that is, by showing us some created good in its lovableness and attractiveness.[53] So, for example, a man's guardian angel might stir up a memory of his mother to deter him from an act that would scandalize her. Angels, holy or fallen, can cause changes in the will by stirring up the passions: pity for the poor man on the Jericho road moves the Samaritan to the act of charity. Even so, there is nothing deterministic about the angelic arousal of our feelings; we have the power to resist.

---

51 *ST* 1a q. 111, a. 1.
52 *ST* 1a q. 111, a. 2.
53 *ST* 1a q. 106, a. 2.

The guardian angels intercede for us with God, and fortify our own feeble attempts to raise mind and heart to heaven. Bossuet encourages us not to be despondent about the poverty of our prayers, because our guardian angels enrich them by their own adoration, thanksgiving, and supplication:

> When you offer God your prayers, how hard you find it to raise your minds to Him! Amidst what storms you struggle to put your intentions into words! How many vain imaginings, how many vague and disordered thoughts, how many temporal cares fling themselves across your path and interrupt your journey! With such impediments, do you really think your prayers can rise up to heaven, that this feeble, languid prayer, beset by a myriad of troubles and hardly emerging out of your hearts, has the power to pierce and penetrate the heights of heaven? Christians, who would believe it? Without doubt they would fall under their own weight, had the goodness of God not made provision for them.... I know that Jesus Christ, in whose name we present our prayers, makes them acceptable. He has sent his angel, whom Tertullian calls the "angel of prayer." This is why Raphael said to Tobias: "I have presented your prayers to God."...This angel comes to gather up our prayers, and, according to St John, they "ascend before God from the hand of the angel" (cf. Apoc 8:4). See how they ascend from the hand of the angel, because this angel, joining himself to us and aiding our feeble prayers, lends them wings to rise, his power to sustain them, his fervor to animate them.[54]

Every human being has a guardian angel. Catholics, non-Catholic Christians, Jews, pagans, all the grand atheists of Hampstead and North Oxford, each of them without exception has at his side a pure spirit, created especially for him, on permanent guard duty. In the Garden of Eden Adam had a good angel to

---

54 J.-B. Bossuet, *Sermon pour la fête des saints anges gardiens, Oeuvres oratoires de Bossuet*, édition critique de l'abbé J. Lebarq, revue et augmentée par C. Urbain & E. Levesque, t. 3 (Paris: Desclée de Brouwer, 1916), 108–9.

protect him, because even in the Garden there was a fallen angel to provoke him. The more we ponder the universality of angelic guardianship, the better we understand that *it belongs to the natural order as well as the supernatural*. God has woven it into the fabric of the world. Angelic guardianship is part of the general condition of men. But don't the angels have a *supernatural* mission? Hasn't God commissioned them to help Christians to remain in, or return to, the state of grace, and finally die in friendship with God and at peace with the Church? Indeed, He has. Surely, then, only the just, souls predestined to grace and glory, should have guardian angels. But no: all men have guardian angels, because, as St Paul says, God wills *all* men to be saved and come to the knowledge of the truth (cf. 1 Tim 2:4), and He gives sufficient grace to all of them, even if that grace, through their own fault, is not efficacious for salvation in every one of them.[55] All men, says St Thomas, are, at least potentially, members of Christ, even though that potentiality will not be actualized in some.[56]

Did Christ our Lord have a guardian angel? According to St Thomas, the divine Word, even as man and on earth, needs no angel to guard Him. In His human soul, on earth and from His conception, He enjoyed the Beatific Vision and was therefore at

---

55 "God is ready to give grace to all. 'He wills all men to be saved, and to come to the knowledge of the truth' (1 Tim 2:40). Those alone are deprived of grace who pose an impediment within themselves to grace; just as, when the sun lights up the world, the man who closes his eyes is held responsible for his fault, if as a result some evil follows, even though he could not see without the sunlight coming first" (*SCG* lib. 3, cap. 152, n. 2). "A just judge antecedently wills all men to live; but consequently wills the murderer to be hanged. Likewise, God antecedently wills all men to be saved, but consequently wills some to be damned, as required by His justice. What we will antecedently, we will not absolutely but with qualifications, for the will is related to things as they are in themselves, and in themselves they exist in a particular way. So we will things absolutely when we have taken all the particularities into consideration; and this is willing consequently. So it can be said that a just judge wills absolutely the hanging of a murderer, but in a qualified way he would want him to live, inasmuch as he is a man. Such a qualified will may be called a willingness rather than an absolute will. Clearly, then, whatever God absolutely wills takes place, but what He wills antecedently may not take place" (*ST* 1a q. 19, a. 6, ad 1).
56 *ST* 3a, q. 8, a. 2.

that high summit of His human nature, already at the goal to which the guardian angel is meant to lead the rest of us. In His human body, subject to suffering as it was, He was a wayfarer, but even there it was not guardian angels but *servant* angels who stood by His side; after the temptations, "the angels ministered to him" (cf Mk 1:13).[57] Some theologians hold that, because of her Immaculate Conception and plenitude of grace, the Blessed Virgin, too, had no guardian angel. Others, more probably in my opinion, argue that, though she was confirmed in grace, Mary Immaculate was not omnipotent, nor on earth did she enjoy beatitude, and so should not have been deprived of a guardian angel, who "would refresh her by his presence and assist her by his ministry."[58]

St Michael was the guardian of the chosen people of Israel, and now he also protects the Church, the New Israel.[59] Particular churches, religious communities, and the provinces and cities of historic Christendom have their special protectors. When he and his cousin entered the Chablais to reconcile its people to the Catholic Church, St Francis de Sales "began by greeting the tutelary angel of the province and recommending to him the great work they were going to undertake."[60] Outside the Winter Palace in St Petersburg is the statue of an angel, holding the cross, on the top of a column. The communists argued for seventy years about which hero of the proletariat should be chosen to replace him. The Marxist system fell before the comrades could agree about whose image should be placed on the plinth, and so the statue of the angel still stands as a sign of the city's safeguarding by God through His angels and His final triumph over evil.

---

57 Cf. *ST* 1a q. 113, a. 4, ad 2.
58 C. R. Billuart, OP, *Cursus theologiae iuxta mentem divi Thomae*, t. 3 (Paris: Mequignon, 1827), 474
59 He is the "prince of the Church, as he was of the Synagogue" (*Super Sententiis* lib. 4, d. 43, q. 1, a. 2, qc. 3, ad 2). According to the seventeenth-century Carmelite theologian João da Sylveira, St Michael is "the guardian, defender, and protector of the Church Militant" (*In Apocalypsim B. Joannis apostoli*, t. 2 [Lyon: 1694], 211).
60 André-Jean-Marie Hamon, *Vie de St Francois de Sales*, abridged ed. (Paris & Lyon: Lecoffre, 1875), 82f.

Dante's Sordello says, in words already quoted, that the holy angels above all protect us from the evil spirit, "for any moment now the Serpent comes."[61] There are many battles with the dark intelligences, many angelic defeats of their attacks, of which we know nothing.

> An immense amount of angelic work for man's benefit must be of the defensive kind; man could never know, unless it were revealed to him, from what evils he has been saved. The spirits fight for us to a great extent without our knowledge, their mission is essentially one of guardianship of a lower being, and it is carried out quite independently of that lower being's participation or recognition. It is truly a trust, and the spirit is responsible for the full discharge of that trust to the heavenly Father by whom it was committed to him.[62]

One moment's reflection on this truth should move us to gratitude to our heavenly Father, and to the angel who applies to the night battles of our souls the victory of the incarnate Son.

DRAWING HIM BACK FROM OTHER EVILS:
THE GUARDIAN ANGEL OF ANTICHRIST

Every man has a guardian angel. The good are guarded, but so, too, are the wicked, even those who to their last breath resist God's grace and thus land themselves in hell, including, according to St Thomas, that most impenitent man, the Antichrist. "The fact that men are lost is not to be imputed to the angels' negligence, but to man's malice."[63] The help God supplies through His angels does not override the freedom He causes in us. The mission of the helping spirits is not to interfere with a man's free decisions, but, in harmony with God's justice and mercy, to diminish the damage his sinful acts inflict upon his fellow men.[64]

---

61 *Purgatorio* 8, 37–39; Sayers, 127.
62 Vonier, *Teaching*, 271.
63 *ST* 1a q. 113, a. 1, ad 3.
64 "The sins of men [explains Abbot Vonier] are no signs that men are not guarded by good spirits, for, as St Thomas says so well [1a q. 113, a. 1, ad 3], we can act against the good instigations of the spirit that is

In the *Commentary on the Sentences*, St Thomas makes two arguments to support his claim that even the Antichrist has a guardian angel:

> The Antichrist, too, will have a guardian angel, because a general law must not be changed in one instance. In this respect [the Antichrist's] punishment will appear more just, because the benefits provided for all of human nature are not withdrawn from him. In any case, the guardianship is not altogether in vain, because, even though he may not be converted to the good, he will cease from inflicting many evils, having been drawn back by his guardian angel, for, by his guardianship, the angel achieves this effect, arguing from the greater to the lesser case, in any man obstinate [in sin].[65]

The first argument—*a general law must not be changed in one instance*—pertains to the Divine Wisdom: an exception in this matter would be a contradiction, and thus an obscuring of the brilliance of Wisdom's ordering of the universe; after all, as we have seen, angelic guardianship belongs to the order of nature. The entailment of Thomas's first argument—*[Antichrist's] punishment will appear more just, because the benefits provided for all of human nature are not withdrawn from him*—reminds us that God's Providence is His justice, as it is also His wisdom and love. The Antichrist, tormented in the eternal flames, has no grounds for protest. Having been blessed by God with his existence and human nature, having had a guardian angel created and appointed to serve him in all good things, he nevertheless

outside us as we can against the good instincts that are within us. The good instincts remain as a great reality in spite of our prevarication; so likewise the angelic inspiration remains in spite of our voluntary deafness to it. Nor could it be said that the spirits work in vain, even with those who are lost. Not only are we to suppose, again with St Thomas [q. 113, a. 4, ad 3], that the most perverted of men are kept from greater evils by their heavenly guardians, but the evil committed by one man is kept in check by those spirits of sanctity, lest it work havoc in other men" (Vonier, *Teaching*, 270f).

65 Cf. St Thomas Aquinas, *Sent.* lib. 2, d. 11, q. 1, a. 3, ad 5.

turns away from God, sets himself up in opposition to God, and dies in self-worshipping impenitence. He has no one but himself to blame for his defeat and damnation. "God [says the *Catechism of the Catholic Church*] predestines no one to go to hell,"[66] not even, so it would seem, the Antichrist.

The second argument — *even though he may not be converted to the good, [Antichrist] will cease from inflicting many evils, having been drawn back by his guardian angel* — reappears, with a little more detail, in the first part of the *Summa*.

> Although angelic guardianship does not help [those foreknown to be eternally lost, including the Antichrist] to merit eternal life by good works, it does help them to be drawn back from certain evils that would hurt both themselves and others. The demons are held off by the good angels, so that they do not do as much harm as they would like to. Likewise Antichrist will not do as much harm as he would like to.[67]

How does the Antichrist's guardian angel "draw him back" from committing even more evil actions than the ones he perpetrates anyway? What we have said already about what angels can and cannot do should help us to offer some speculative answers to the question. Since guardian angels can bring about changes in material things, Antichrist's angel might ground the plane taking him to the place where he would have proclaimed some outrageous heresy. With his power to excite emotions, the angel might arouse even in Antichrist's heart a natural pity that would hold him back from murdering those who oppose him. A similar interpretation can be applied to St Paul's statement that the Antichrist is "restrained" until the appointed time of his appearing (cf. 2 Thess 2:6). After his birth, and before he strides onto the stage of human history to do the devil's work, he is held in check by the holy angels of God, including his own guardian angel. Under angelic restraint, within the purposes of

---

66   CCC 1037.
67   *ST* 1a q. 113, a. 4, ad 3.

Divine Providence, his subversion of the true religion of Christ lasts less time than it might have done.

The Antichrist *does* have a guardian angel. That truth helps us to understand better the death-dealing office of the Antichrist and the life-giving ministry of the holy bodiless spirits. It sheds light on the Catholic doctrines of Creation, Providence, and the Last Things. It reminds us that human history, in the disasters of all times and the horrors of the last times, is *not out of control.*[68] The provident God does not will, either directly or indirectly, the sinful actions of men, even those of that most wicked man, the Antichrist, but He does permit them to happen, because He knows how to bring good out of the evil that men do. The good that by Divine Providence comes out of the evil done by Antichrist is the final victory of the true Christ, the conqueror of death, and the triumph of the Immaculate Heart of His ever-virgin Mother, the Queen of the Angels.

Our angel's task is to get us to heaven. Like many of the Doctors, St Bernard argues that, through the help our guardian angels give us on the way to salvation, we fill the gaps in heaven left by the apostate angels. He addresses the blessed spirits:

> We do not think that you, citizens of heaven, take pleasure in the ruining of your city, and the wrecking of its walls, which, as you can see, are half-demolished. If you really want the city to be restored, as is right, then again and again repeat before the throne of glory, I beg you, this prayer: "Be kind in thy good will, O Lord, to Zion, that the walls of Jerusalem be built up." If you love the beauty of God's house, or rather since you do love it, let your zeal be felt by the living and rational stones, who alone can be built up with you for the city's restoration.[69]

---

68 "This spiritual tutelage is meant above all things to keep the human race and human individuals in the perfection of nature, and we may say without any exaggeration that the human race would have succumbed long ago to enemies, to deleterious influences, but for the ever-protecting, divinely directed activity of those benign powers" (Vonier, *Teaching,* 270).
69 St Bernard, *In festo Sancti Michaelis, Sermo* 1, n. 4; PL 183.449C. Cf. St Augustine, *Enchiridion* cap. 29; PL 40.246.

⇀⇀

GODWARD IS THE HOLY ANGELS' GAZE, AND
Godward they lead us by what they do amid the stars and for
our souls:

> Upward all these orders gaze with awe,
>> and downward are with us so bound
>> that all to God are drawn and to Him draw.[70]

70　*Paradiso* 28, 127–29; author's translation.

BOTTICELLI, INFERNO 34

4

THE · REBEL · BAND

THE FALLEN ANGELS AND OUR SPIRITUAL COMBAT WITH THEM

I N THE TWENTY-NINTH CANTO OF THE *Paradiso*, the smiling Beatrice continues her lecture on the angels:

> Count up twenty; thou wilt be too slow—
>   Even faster did one angel band rebel
>   And bring convulsion to the earth below.[1]

There are faithful angels, and there are fallen angels. Most angels are in heaven, but many are in hell. God created all the angels to be good, of whom some by their own free act made themselves evil. This rebel band of ruined spirits is the devil (Satan or Lucifer) and his demons. Adam sinned at their incitement, and now they are permitted by God to tempt us, Adam's children, into joining their revolt against God. They are tireless foes of our race and nature; to our last breath, we must do battle with them in the power of the risen Christ. "Brethren, be sober and watch, because your adversary the devil, as a roaring lion, goeth about, seeking whom he may devour: whom resist ye, strong in faith" (1 Pt 5:8f). In the last of his drawings for the *Inferno*, Botticelli uses two sheets of vellum to confront us "with the horror of Satan, 'Emperor of the Universe of Pain.'"[2]

---

1 *Paradiso* 29, 49–51; Sayers-Reynolds, 310.
2 George Robinson, notes on *Inferno*, canto 34, in Kenneth Clark, *The Drawings by Sandro Botticelli for Dante's Divine Comedy*, 82.

CHALLENGED TO SELF-GIVING LOVE:
THE TESTING OF THE ANGELS

The first moment of the angels' existence in the participated eternity of "aeviternity,"[3] if we could experience it, would seem like many days of rich eventfulness.[4] It was the springtime of God's creation. Adam came into existence in a visible world already shaken by the fall of the angels, and in a garden whose loveliness was lessened by the lurking of the Serpent. But no shadow of sin darkened the angels' first state. The nature of the bodiless spirits, as it came from the hands of God, was intact and beautiful, their hierarchies strong and complete. Each angel in his station possessed, from the beginning of his existence, a natural knowledge vast in scope and brilliant in perception; his will was on fire with the surging natural love proper to a bodiless spirit. There was nothing, in this first age-like instant, to distinguish those who would fall from those who would be faithful. Even now, after the fall, if we consider only the nature of the angels, there is nothing to mark off a holy angel from a demon. Sin is the only respect in which they differ, and it is the difference of eternal bliss and everlasting damnation. Rebellion is what changes Lucifer, the bearer of light, into the bringer of darkness; pride and disobedience turn a spirit filled by his Creator with truth into the father of lies. "All day long he multiplies lies and desolation" (Hos 12:1). The divine playwright did not write this catastrophe into the drama of salvation. It arises from the improvisation of the actors, angels and men, and is then controlled by God, who brings good out of the evil His creatures do.[5] With the same thought in mind, Abbot Vonier asks us to consider the different ways in which our Lord speaks of the happiness of heaven and the misery of hell.

---

3   See *ST* 1a q. 10, a. 5, and 66 above.
4   "One angelic instant can last hours and days in our time, just as the saints, in contemplating the same object, can spend many hours in ecstasy." Reginald Garrigou-Lagrange, OP, *De Deo trino et creatore: Commentarius in Summa theologicam S. Thomae (1a qq. 27–119)* (Turin: Marietti, 1943), 367.
5   Jacques Maritain speaks of "the improvisations of nothingness of created existents." *God and the Permission of Evil* (Milwaukee: Bruce, 1966), 113.

THE · REBEL · BAND

When Christ speaks of the reward of the elect, he
represents it in the form of an invitation to take possession of the Kingdom that had been prepared from
the foundation of the world. The chastisement of the
wicked he speaks of as everlasting fire prepared for the
devil and his angels. This terrible penal arrangement is
not said to be, like the gracious provision for merit, *a
constitutione mundi*, from the foundation of the world.
Satan and his followers were not created evil; there was
no thought in God's first providence of an *ignis aeternus*.
No Christian doubts the existence of evil powers in
the spirit world, but no Christian considers those evil
powers to be anything but a miscarriage, through the
creature's act, of the Creator's first plan. There is no
evil principle having, so to speak, an estate by itself;
all evil is an apostasy of a being that was primarily
good; all evil is a bad use of the good things of God.[6]

There is no evil principle. Whatever is now evil was good when it
came from the hands of God. "The demons were not created as
such, as the name 'demons' might suggest, for God made nothing
evil. The demons, too, were created good, but, having fallen from
heavenly wisdom, they now prowl round the earth and deceive the
heathen by their illusions."[7] The first state of the angels was very
good indeed in both natural endowments and supernatural enrich-
ments. Nothing was lacking in what by nature they were; their
intellects had been filled by God with a vast store of knowledge.
The angels, newly created, were naturally satisfied and at peace.
But they did not possess the ultimate, supernatural happiness
of seeing God, One and Triune, "as He is" (cf. 1 Jn 3:2), for that
final goal lies beyond the natural constitution and powers of any
creature.[8] You cannot fall from the supernatural fulfilment of your
nature; once attained in the Beatific Vision, the Supreme Good
cannot lose its appeal. But you can turn from the path leading

---

6   Vonier, *Teaching*, 276. Among the ideas of things pre-existing in the mind
of God, there is no idea of evil: "Evil is known by God, not through its own
definition, but through the definition of the good. There is no idea of evil in
God, neither as exemplary cause nor as definition" (*ST* 1a q. 15, a. 3, ad 1).
7   St Athanasius, *Vita S. Antonii*, 22; PG 26.876AB.
8   Cf. *ST* 1a q. 62, a. 1.

to the final goal and head off in the opposite direction. Such a deviation is what mortal sin is, first in angels and then in men.

According to St Thomas, following the teaching of the Fathers,[9] the angels were created, not with glory, but with sanctifying grace, the "seed" of glory.[10] They were required to merit the state of glory by a free act informed by grace and charity.[11] The Triune God freely and generously decreed supernatural beatitude for them, but, in His wise and loving plan, they could not attain the goal without passing a test. For the angels, as for men, the clear vision of God was to be the reward of proven fidelity. Before sharing in the knowing and loving of the Three Divine Persons through face-to-face vision and beatific love, the angels had to make the free gift of themselves to God in charity. This act of soaring away from self to God, the great ecstasy and adventure of the creature made in God's image, some of the angels refused to make.

By their first act of charity the angels merited eternal bliss, and immediately possessed it; they began to behold God face-to-face, and to share His happiness forever, "innumerable angels in festal gathering" (cf Heb 12:2). The supernatural perfects and presupposes nature. Now the angels by nature do nothing by a slow and gradual process, but with swift and immediate perfection. Therefore, "the angel became blessed immediately after a single act informed by charity."[12] Meanwhile, the other angels, puffed up with self, turned away from God, and were immediately lost in eternal darkness. "God did not spare the angels when they sinned but cast them into hell and committed them to pits of nether gloom" (2 Pt 2:4). Those once good by nature and grace became bad beyond redemption. "In the first instant the angels were all good, but in a second they divided into good and evil."[13]

---

9 "Nothing is sanctified without the presence of the Holy Spirit...[to the angels] the Holy Spirit imparted sanctification" (St Basil the Great, *In psalmos homiliae* 32, n. 4; PG 29.333).

10 Cf. *ST* 1a q. 62, a. 3.

11 Cf. *ST* 1a q. 62, a. 4. "It was not by a natural turning [to God] that the angel merited beatitude, but by the turning that is charity, through grace" (ad 2).

12 *ST* 1a q. 62, a. 5.

13 *ST* 1a q. 63, a. 6, ad 4.

"BY THE FORCE OF GRAVITY":
THE FALL OF THE ANGELS

No intellectual creature is incapable of sin in every respect and all states of its nature. St Thomas supplies the proof. You can only be impeccable if your will is the rule in every case to be followed; then whatever you will, whatever end you pursue, is the right thing to do. But only God has such a will, because there is no higher end, no greater good, than He who is the supreme and infinite Good. Therefore, every created will, if left to its own powers, can sin.[14] Christ our Lord was impeccable, even as man; His human will could not sin; but this impeccability was caused by the union of human nature with the divine person of the Word, and from the supernatural perfections consequent upon the union.[15] Our Lady was free from all sin, original and actual, mortal and venial, immune even from the inclination to sin,[16] but that perfect purity of soul was the effect of a singular grace and privilege bestowed upon her by God and merited by His and her Son with His human will. The blessed in heaven cannot sin, but such sinlessness has a supernatural cause: the glorification of their wills and their participation in God's own faultless freedom. They are so divinely free they are free from the possibility of sinning.

Granted that no creature can be *absolutely* incapable of sin, and that, having been elevated to the supernatural order, some of the angels did sin, could the angels have sinned if God had created them in a state of pure nature? Is the possibility of sinning inherent in the angels' creatureliness, or do they become capable of falling only when they are raised to a state surpassing their nature?

---

14 Cf. *ST* 1a q. 61, a. 1.

15 *Sent.* lib. 3, d. 12, q. 2, a. 1.

16 "The consequences of the privilege of the Immaculate Conception are especially the following. The Blessed Virgin Mary never had the *fomes peccati* [the 'tinder of sin,' the inclination to sin]; there were never disordered involuntary movements of the sense appetites in her; there was always a perfect subordination of the sense appetites to the intellect and to a will always subject to God's good pleasure, as in the state of innocence." Reginald Garrigou-Lagrange, OP, *Mariologiae compendium*, in *De Christo Salvatore: Commentarius in IIIam partem* Summa theologicae *sancti Thomae* (Turin & Rome: Marietti, 1949), 506.

On this question Thomists disagree with each other.[17] Here is a Dominican voice in defense of a natural impeccability in the angel:

> For St Thomas [said Fr Garrigou-Lagrange], by a natural love the angel loves more than himself not only beatitude in general, but also God, the author of his nature. Therefore, it is more probable that he cannot directly and immediately sin again his natural law, which he intuitively sees written into his own nature. But the demon by directly and immediately sinning against the *supernatural* law sinned indirectly against the natural law.[18]

By contrast, Jacques Maritain argues that the notion of a naturally impeccable creature involves a contradiction. "The creature as such cannot be free unless it be free in a freedom that is kindred to nothingness (because it is the freedom of a creature drawn from nothingness), in a freedom, therefore, which, as to the natural order, may be subject to failure; this surely must be clear—a free creature, naturally impeccable, would be a squared circle."[19]

St Thomas makes a similar argument to Maritain's in the disputed questions *De veritate*. The subjects of natures without reason are ordered towards particular goods: the lion toward its prey for food and toward its lioness for mating. But the subjects of rational natures, persons, are ordered toward the good in an absolute sense; their wills are made for the good, as their intellects are made for truth. So the actions of the rational creature are not determined to follow one course rather than another on the way to the goal; the rational creature can freely *choose* the path that he judges will lead him to the good. Now actions have a likeness to the agent: fire heats. If the action is to be unvarying, if the heat is to remain at the same temperature day and night,

---

17   See Jacques Maritain, "Le péché de l'ange. Essai de réinterprétation des positions thomistes," in Charles Journet, Jacques Maritain, & Philippe de la Trinité, *Le péché de l'ange: Peccabilité, nature et surnature* (Paris: Beauchesne, 1961), 41–86; Joseph-Marie Gilliot, "Comment l'ange peut pécher: Réflexions autour d'un débat du XXe siècle," in *Sedes sapientiae* 152 (2020), 35–54.
18   Reginald Garrigou-Lagrange, OP, *De Deo trino et creatore*, 353.
19   Jacques Maritain, *St Thomas and the Problem of Evil* (Milwaukee: Marquette University Press, 1942), 15.

then the agent, too, must be unvarying; the fire must have the same force day and night; there can be no cooling of the embers. Likewise, if the actions of a rational nature, which is ordered to the good absolutely, are to be always perfectly good, the nature itself must be perfectly and absolutely good. St Thomas concludes:

> God alone is pure act with no mixture of potentiality, and for this reason is pure and absolute goodness. But every creature, since it is mixed up with potentiality in its nature, is a particular good. And it is mixed up with potentiality because it comes from nothing. Therefore, among rational natures only God has a free will that is naturally impeccable and confirmed in the good. Such impeccability is impossible in a creature because, as Damascene and Gregory of Nyssa say, *it is from nothing.*[20]

NO SECOND CHANCE:
THE OBSTINACY OF THE FALLEN ANGELS

If an angel sins, the sin must be mortal. The intuition of his mind sees the means in the end, and the end in the means, and so he cannot turn away from the due means to an end without turning from the ultimate end, thereby sinning mortally.[21] Having sinned, the demons remain obstinate in evil. There is no second chance for the fallen angels, no possibility of repentance

---

20   St Thomas, *De veritate* q. 24, a. 7. In other places St Thomas seems to hold a different opinion: the angel is fallible, not because he is a creature and close to nothing, but because he is an intellectual creature elevated to the supernatural order: "Just as we [men] do not change in our knowledge of first principles, so [the angels'] intellect does not change with regard to what they know naturally; and as the will is proportioned to the intellect, it follows that their will, too, is naturally immutable with regard to what belongs to the natural order. But they are in potency in the sense that they can change with regard to supernatural goods, by turning to them or turning away from them. So the only change that can happen to them is that they move from the level of their nature to what surpasses their nature, by turning to these goods or turning away from them" (*De malo* q. 16, a. 5). Père Hyacinthe Dondaine, OP, resolves the apparent contradiction between this text in the *De malo* and the texts from the *Summa theologiae* by arguing that St Thomas changed his mind between his work on the *Prima pars* and his writing of the *De malo*. "Le premier instant de l'ange d'après saint Thomas," *Revue des sciences philosophiques et théologiques* 39 (1955), 213–27.
21   Cf. *ST* 1a q. 63, a. 3.

and redemption. The opinion of Origen, who maintained that in some future universal restoration the demons would be converted, is to be rejected as heresy, for it presupposes that every created will (apart from that of Christ), whatever its state, can turn to either good or evil. But such a view would entail not only that the demons in hell can repent, but that the blessed in heaven can rebel, a conclusion that denies the very nature of beatitude as everlasting, unchangeable, and secure.[22] The demons are likewise permanently fixed in their sin and consequently in the fire of their eternal torment (cf. Mt 25:41). As St Thomas says, quoting St John Damascene, the fall of the angels was what death is for us: the end of the opportunity for conversion and forgiveness.[23]

The obstinacy of the demons has its cause not outside them (as if, for example, God denied them the grace of repentance) but deep within, in the way in which by nature they as angels will. "It is the irrevocable character of their choice [says the *Catechism*], and not a defect in the infinite divine mercy, that makes the angels' sin unforgivable."[24] The power of will is proportionate to the power of mind: as you know and understand, so you desire and will, because you can only desire something that somehow you know. Human beings know, think, and understand in a step-by-step process, and we make our choices with similar complexity and long-windedness. We weigh up the considerations, perhaps list them, pro and con: shall I, shan't I? Now, as we have seen, the angels know and understand by way of intuition, which is a kind of mental seeing. So the angel sees what he wills with total penetration, and then wills it with utter conviction. Therefore, having made his evil choice, the demon remains fixed in evil. You can't say to him after he has sinned, "But why didn't you consider this or that?" He considered everything, and nothing gave him pause. Once set in a certain direction, the angel's will cannot turn back: its acts are swift, complete, and perpetually enduring. *Count up twenty—thou wilt be too slow,/ Even faster did*

---

22 Cf. St Thomas, *De veritate* q. 24, a. 8.
23 Cf. *ST* 1a q. 64, a. 2.
24 CCC 393.

one Angel band rebel. For good or ill, in what he chooses and does, the angel is not a laggard.

Abbot Vonier sums up the eternal state of the devil and his demons:

> Satan and his followers are truly cast out into eternal darkness, into the fire which will be their prison forever. They are darkened in their intellects with regard to the mysteries of grace, with regard to the counsels of God's free will, but not with regard to things which constitute the glories of the natural universe; the knowledge of the natural universe is part of their very being, and they could not lose it without losing their identity.[25]

"ACCURSED PRIDE": THE SIN OF THE ANGELS

Angelic sin is not impossible, but it seems improbable. In creating the bodiless spirits, God filled their intellects with a wonderful fullness of knowledge, and so they could not sin by ignorance or error. Their wills, following their intellects, could not choose evil, thinking it was good. However, they could choose good in an unruly, immoderate, and thus sinful way, and that is what they did.[26] "Of his own free will the angel sinned by pursuing his own good without respect for the rule of God's will."[27] We, too, can do good things in a bad way: for example, it is good to go to church to pray, but if you say your prayers in a booming voice and deafen the other people in the pews, you are out of order and therefore sinning, at least venially. Visiting the sick is a corporal work of mercy, but if you overstay your welcome and wear out the invalid with your chatter, you are doing more harm than good.

The angels have no bodies, and so cannot fall into bodily sins such as fornication and drunkenness; their sins, like their nature, will be entirely spiritual.[28] As pure spirits, they can be drawn only to spiritual goods. Now the fallen angels loved a spiritual good in a disordered way, without observing the rule imposed by One

---

25 Vonier, *Teaching*, 278.
26 Cf. *ST* 1a q. 63, a. 1, ad 4.
27 Cf. ibid.
28 Cf. *ST* 1a q. 63, a. 2.

higher than they, their Creator. But not submitting to the rule of your superior, when submission is due, is to be proud. Therefore, the angels sinned by pride. Dante says through Beatrice:

> The prime cause of the fall was the accursed
> pride of the angel whom you saw beneath
> all the weight of the cosmos, crushed and pressed.[29]

This teaching is what we find in the writings of the wise man and the Apostle. "Pride is the beginning of all sin," says the son of Sirach (Ecclus 10:13). Likewise, the reason St Paul gives for not allowing recent converts to be bishops is to prevent them getting "puffed up with pride" and "falling into the judgment of the devil" (cf 1 Tim 3:6), that is, to be judged and condemned for sinful pride, as the devil was.[30]

We catch an echo of Satan's own sin in the words he uses to tempt our first parents: "You will be like God" (Gen 3:5).[31] "Puffed up with arrogance (*elatione inflatus*)," says St Augustine, Lucifer "wanted to be called God."[32] St Thomas says that the devil wanted to be like God, but not by nature and in equality, for he knew by his natural intelligence that such a pretension was impossible: no creature can rank with his Creator.

> It is natural for an intelligence or separated intellect to understand its own substance; and thus he naturally knew that his being was imparted by someone higher. Now natural knowledge in him was not corrupted by sin. Therefore, the devil's intellect could not grasp the equality of himself with God under the aspect of the possible. But no one aims at what he sees as impossible.... Therefore, it is impossible that the movement of the devil's will would aim at attaining absolute equality with God.... He

29 *Paradiso* 29, 55–57; Esolen 313.
30 "When someone coming new to the faith is promoted to some position, he thinks himself better than other people and very necessary to them, as if, unless he were there, they would lack the wherewithal to provide for the Church. He says 'of the devil,' because he was condemned for the sin of pride" (St Thomas, *Super 1 Timotheum* cap. 3, lect. 2).
31 Cf. CCC 392.
32 *Quaestiones ex veteri testamento* 2; PL 35.2216.

could not desire not to be absolutely subject to God, both because this is impossible and because he would cease to exist if he were not totally subject to God.[33]

There is another sense in which desiring to be like God is possible for the angels. Since intellectual creatures, angels and men, are made by God in His likeness, their aspiration to resemble Him more closely is in itself not sinful, but admirable; after all, our Lord commands us to be "perfect as [our] heavenly Father is perfect" (Mt 5:48). But there is a condition on the aspiration: the goal must be pursued as a *gift* freely bestowed by God. If you desire Godlikeness as something you think you can claim from God in justice, or can attain by your own powers, then your desire is sinful.

> In this way the devil desired to be like God. He did *not* desire to be like God by being subject to absolutely no one else, for that would mean his desiring non-existence, since no creature can exist except by partaking of existence under God. But he did desire to be like God in the following way: he desired as his final goal of beatitude *something he could attain by the power of his own nature*, thus turning his desire away from supernatural beatitude, which comes from God's grace. Or, another possibility, if he desired as his final goal the likeness to God that is a gift of grace, he wanted to have this by the power of his own nature, and not with God's help according to His ordinance.... These two views of the devil's fall in a way come down to the same thing, since, according to both, he sought to have final beatitude through his own power, whereas this is proper to God alone.[34]

This overrating of himself explains Lucifer's desire to dominate the universe: "Since what exists *through itself* is the ruler and cause of whatever exists *through another*, the devil's sin was also a desire to rule other things; in this way, too, he desired to be like God."[35]

---

33 St Thomas, *De malo* q. 16, a. 3.
34 *ST* 1a q. 63, a. 3.
35 *ST* 1a q. 63, a. 3.

In the demons, as in the despots and dictators, the obsession with one's own powers and the desire for their extension are born of pride in the form of *vanity*. The devil "did not refer his own good to the divine good,"[36] but absorbed himself entirely in contemplation of the force and splendor of his own nature. "The sight of his own beauty and eminence having made him fall in love with himself and his private good [says St Bonaventure], he presumed upon the lofty state already his to aspire to a further height he did not possess."[37]

---

36 *SCG* lib. 3, cap. 110, n. 3. "In this way did the angel sin, because he turned his free will to his own good without reference to the [higher] rule of the divine will" (*ST* 1a q. 63, a. 1, ad 4). "Knowing themselves and all the excellence bestowed on them from above, [the fallen angels] did not refer themselves back to the Creator with humble recognition and true gratitude, but having vain complacency in themselves, they desired their own honor, preferring to live and reign according to their own will than to subject themselves in an orderly way and be moderated and governed by His law and rule. Hence, properly speaking, their sin was *ambition*, which contains and includes the turning of their minds away from God, vain complacency in themselves, and negligence of due consideration and the relation of themselves and their gifts to the primal fount, the most munificent God" (Blessed Denys the Carthusian, DCOO 33. 173AB). "The natural greatness of the angel is a glory which has no equal; it is a singular perfection which is without a rival. A spirit may thus choose to enter into communion with the supernatural or to remain entirely in his own sphere, preferring his own natural excellency to the communion of the universal family of God. St Thomas says that some spirits chose the second alternative; they preferred their natural glory in its isolation to the community of the supernatural charity; and this is the fall of the angels. It is pride — because they elected excellency without reference to the more excellent good; it is rebellion — because the Will of God was that they should accept the supernatural; it is envy — not in the sense of the dark human passion, but in the sense of an opposition to a holy thing, the grace of God. All other sins must be taken more or less metaphorically in the case of the fallen angels" (Vonier, *Teaching*, 277).

37 St Bonaventure, *Breviloquium* 2, 7; *Sancti Bonaventurae opera omnia*, vol. 5 (Quaracchi, 1891), 225. "Lucifer was adorned with divine radiance, and outshone the power of heaven through the Creator's gift, but came to believe that the splendid wisdom and beautiful virtue which God's grace had bestowed on him was the result of his own natural ability, not a gift from God's goodness. Preening himself on this, as if he needed no divine help in maintaining his pure state, he considered himself equal to God, as if like God he had no need of any other; overconfident in his freedom of will, he thought that would be enough to supply him for all he needed for perfect virtue and perpetual happiness. That single thought of his was the primal fall." St John Cassian, *The Monastic Institutes: Consisting of On the Training of a Monk and The Eight Deadly Sins in Twelve Books*, ed. and trans. Fr Jerome Bertram, Cong. Orat. (London: St Austin Press, 1999), 14f.

The devil's sin against the good, grace, and charity was also a sin against the truth. Pride is a lie. Our Lord says of the devil that "he stood not in the truth, because truth is not in him" (Jn 8:44). "He abandoned the order of his nature [says St Thomas], which was that he be subject to God, and through [God] acquire his happiness and the fulfillment of his natural desire. But, because he wanted to obtain [that fulfilment] through himself, he fell from the truth."[38]

On the heels of the angels' pride followed envy. We envy someone when we are distressed at his wellbeing, because we feel it to be an impediment to our own, or an insult to our sense of superiority: "He got the job, but I was much better qualified."

> So it was with the evil angel. The only reason he saw someone else's good as a hindrance to the good he desired was that he desired an *unrivalled* excellence, which would cease to be unrivalled if someone else had it as well. So, after the sin of pride, there followed the evil of envy in the sinning angel, by which he grieved over man's good, and even over the excellence of God inasmuch as against the devil's will God makes use of man for the divine glory.[39]

The demons' frustration, their envy of what men can still attain but they have lost irrevocably, is the driving force in their work of temptation. They "envy man," says Scheeben, "the heavenly treasure they have lost, and ... seek to enmesh [man] in their insurrection and their fall, so that he might not succeed to the place in heaven from which they have been ejected."[40] They are proud toward God, and envious toward us, and by their envy try to draw us into the mortal sin that robs us of the divine life of grace. In this sense, as our Lord tells us, the devil was "a murderer from the beginning" (cf. Jn 8:44). "By the devil's envy, death came

---

38 St Thomas Aquinas, *Super Ioannem* cap. 8, lec. 6.
39 *ST* 1a q. 63, a. 2. "Since he did not 'stand in the truth' (cf. Jn 8:44), and by his pride lost all the glory of his nature, [the devil] bewails man's restoration by the mercy of God and his being ushered into the goods he himself [the devil] has lost" (St Leo the Great, *Sermo 48, De Quadragesima* 10, cap. 2; PL 54.299A).
40 Scheeben, *The Mysteries of Christianity*, 267.

into the world" (Wis 2:24). Satan kills Adam and Eve, and then every man who succumbs to his tempting, "not as if he were armed with a sword, but by evil persuasion."[41] A murderous man kills the body, but the devil can kill the soul "by drawing us into mortal sin and so taking away the life of grace."[42]

According to St Thomas, who here follows the opinion of St Gregory the Great, the highest of the angels to fall was the greatest of all.[43] But was he the very highest of all the angels created by God, or just the highest in a certain order? After all, the higher angels, with their superior perfection of intellect and will, would seem less prone to sin than the lower. St John Damascene therefore argued that the greatest of the sinning angels was greatest *only among the lower angels "set over the earthly order,"* that is, the ones who serve God in the government of the visible universe. But St Thomas points out that, if you look at the motive for sinning, the higher angels were the more likely to sin. The devil's sin was an act of pride, and the motive of someone's pride is his excellence. Now Lucifer had the greatest excellence in which to glory, and he did so glory, in contempt of the God from whom he received everything he had and was. Thus, the best, once corrupted by his pride, became the worst.[44] St Thomas suggests that Lucifer was in fact the highest of the Cherubim, who excel in knowledge, whereas the Seraphim above them are on fire with charity.[45] The highest of the angels to fall was a grand intellectual.

St Hildegard describes the terrible change in Satan and the other rebellious angels from light into darkness: "By the command of the almighty Father, the angel Lucifer, who is now Satan, was adorned at his creation with great glory and came forth with much brilliance and attired in beauty, and with him all the sparks of his retinue. Then they were dazzling white in the brightness of light, but now they shine no more in the gloom of night."[46]

---

41 Cf. *Super Ioannem* cap. 8, lect. 6.
42 Cf. St Thomas Aquinas, *De decem praeceptis* a. 7.
43 "He was set over all the angelic hosts, and by comparison surpassed them in glory" (St Gregory the Great, *Homilia* 34, n. 7; PL 76.1250BC).
44 Cf. *ST* 1a q. 63, a. 7.
45 Cf. *ST* 1a q. 63, a. 7, ad 1.
46 St Hildegard, *Scivias* pars 3, visio 1, cap. 14; CCCM 43A.341f.

The corruption of the best is the worst, and the disfiguring of the most beautiful is the ugliest. But the pure spirituality of the angelic nature has a greater likeness to the infinite goodness and beauty of God than does the nature of any bodily creature. The devil is therefore, in his pride and obstinacy, hideous beyond description.[47]

Having fallen, Lucifer brought down other angels with him. These were to be his soldiers, or rather his slaves, for, as St Peter says, "by whom a man is overcome, of the same also is he a slave" (2 Pt 2:19). Angels do not ponder and deliberate, nor is there a pause between an angel's thinking of a bad thought and his articulation of it. "So, in the same instant in which the chief angel expressed the state of his will to the other angels by intelligible speech, it was possible for the other angels to consent to it."[48] Their motive was the same as his: the attainment of ultimate bliss by their natural powers. They fell into line with him, because already in the natural order they were subject to him.[49] St Thomas assures us that a greater number of angels stayed faithful than rebelled: "There are more with them than with us" (4 Kgs 6:16). Since sin is against the deepest inclination of nature, it happens only in a minority of cases, "for nature produces its effect either always or more often than not." Therefore, it is improbable that a majority of creatures endowed by God with a sublime natural perfection of intellect and will would fall into the folly and self-destruction of sin.[50]

Some masters of sacred doctrine have claimed that if the mystery of the Incarnation was revealed to the created spirits in their first state, their rebellious act of pride was a refusal, in advance, to adore and obey God the Son in His human nature: *Non serviam* ("I will not serve," cf. Jer 2:20, Vulg.). Lucifer, in his lofty spirituality, would not worship his Creator, God Most High, in lowly human flesh.

---

47 Cf. Matthias J. Scheeben, *Die Herrlichkeiten der göttlichen Gnade, Gesammelte Schriften*, Band 1 (Freiburg: Herder, 1949), 110.
48 *ST* 1a q. 63, a. 8, ad 1.
49 *ST* 1a q. 63, a. 8, ad 2.
50 Cf. *ST* 1a q. 63, a. 9.

Can the sin of the angels be more naturally explained [asks Scheeben], and the malice of their insurrection more profoundly represented, than in this hypothesis? If an angel, especially the most brilliant of all, Lucifer, became absorbed in the contemplation of his glorious nature, and conceived the idea that God preferred human nature to this lofty nature, and even made him dependent on a man for his own highest and noblest prerogative, might he not have been wroth that God had passed his nature by, must he not have burned with envy of the favored human race, and above all must he not have been consumed with ungovernable hatred against the Son of Man, to whom he had to pay homage, whom he was bid to adore? ... The most monstrous and the blackest of all crimes, and at the same time most inconceivable of all, deicide, resulted inevitably from the angel's rebellion, and accounts for the frightful malignity manifested in its purpose.[51]

"ENEMY OF THE HUMAN RACE": HERESY AND THE HATRED OF MAN

The devil, says St Peter, is "our *adversary*" (cf. 1 Pt 5:8) — *our* adversary. Peter's successors St Leo I and St Gregory I likewise call him "the enemy of the human race."[52] The fallen angel's hostility towards humanity is born of his pride and envy, and of his contempt for all that is bodily, including and especially the true human body of God the Son, born of the Virgin Mary. Now the devil's despising of the flesh has been replicated through the centuries by the heresies of Gnosticism, Manichaeism, and Albigensianism, which regard everything bodily as evil, the material order as the work of a malevolent deity, and the Incarnation as an illusion. Such errors were even propagated in the age of the apostles. The mark of the devil's henchman, the Antichrist, says St John, is his denial that "Jesus Christ has come *in the flesh*"

---

51 Scheeben, *The Mysteries of Christianity*, 269–70.
52 ... *inimicus humani generis* (St Leo the Great, *Sermo* 69, *De passione Domini* 18, cap. 3; PL 54.377C); *hostis humani generis* (St Gregory the Great, *Moralium liber* 33, cap. 7; PL 76.680D).

(1 Jn 4:3). St Ignatius of Antioch, disciple of the apostles, describes the bodily mysteries of the virginity of Mary, her childbirth, and her divine Son's Death on the Cross as "hidden from the prince of this world":[53] they elude his mind's natural powers and so thwart his mighty and unruly will.

The Modernism and Neo-Modernism of the twentieth and twenty-first centuries manifest the same Luciferian disdain for the flesh of the Word with its skepticism about the truths of divine revelation pertaining to the body: the virginity of Mary (in conceiving, in giving birth, and forever after giving birth), the miracles of Christ, His Resurrection from the dead *secundum carnem*, and the changing of the whole substance of bread and wine into His Body and Blood in the Eucharistic mystery. For the Modernist, Christianity is not a religion revealed by God in time and space, in the history of Israel, and finally "in the fulness of time," in the human words, sufferings, and actions of God's only-begotten Son, the Word made flesh, born of woman (cf. Gal 4:4; Heb 1:2), but an interior, purely spiritual experience, the "religious sentiment."[54] The Modernist does not preach the Gospel of the Word of life, who was seen on earth by human eyes and touched with human hands (cf. 1 Jn 1:1). He prefers a religion more spiritual and impalpable, a preference that is pleasing to the arrogant angel who is hostile to everything human.

ANGELISM

The father of lies encourages every assault on truth, be it revealed or attainable by reason. Angelism, the delusion of the man who thinks he is essentially an angel and only accidentally and inconveniently the possessor of a body, is a notion particularly attractive to his perverted angelic intelligence. It is a doctrine that has afflicted many of the philosophies of the modern age, beginning, as Jacques Maritain has argued, with Descartes: "Let

53 St Ignatius of Antioch, *Epistola ad Ephesios*, cap. 19; J. B. Lightfoot, *The Apostolic Fathers: Revised Texts with Short Introductions and English Translations* (London: Macmillan, 1885), 141f.
54 Cf. St Pius X, *Pascendi dominici gregis*, Encyclical on the Doctrines of the Modernists (1907), n. 8.

us try to find the right names for things: the sin of Descartes is a sin of *angelism*. He turned knowledge and thought into a hopeless perplexity, an abyss of unrest, because he conceived human thought after the type of angelic thought. To sum it up in three words: What he saw in man's thought was *independence of things*."[55] The three notes of angelic knowledge are that it is "intuitive as to its mode, innate as to its origin, independent of things as to its nature."[56] These, according to Descartes, are the very attributes of human knowledge. He wants to free philosophy from "the burden of discursive reasoning." To "the laborious farrago of the School and its swarm of syllogisms" he opposes "a ready, distinct, level science, a sheet of clearness."[57] Man does not sully his mind with concepts drawn from his sense-experience of the visible world. He is born with a stock of ideas deriving from his Creator. "The Cartesian ideas come from God, like angelic ideas, not from objects. Thus, the human soul is not only subsistent as the ancients taught, causing the body with its own existence; it has, without the body, received direct from God all the operative perfection which can befit it."[58]

Now, according to Maritain, the angelism of Descartes has a fatal consequence for the intellectual, moral, and political history of the West: the soul's good is reduced to "the domination of the physical universe."[59] The man who sees himself as essentially spiritual and his body as a machine that he occupies and controls will see the entire bodily order as a vast apparatus to be exploited and manipulated.

> This universe, the whole of which has not the value of one spirit, will make it pay dear for this disordering. This angel is iron-gloved, and extends its sovereign action over the corporeal world by the innumerable arms of Machinery. Poor angel turning the grindstone,

---

55 Jacques Maritain, *Three Reformers: Luther, Descartes, Rousseau* (London: Sheed & Ward, 1950), 54f.
56 Ibid., 57
57 Ibid.
58 Ibid., 63.
59 Ibid., 64.

enslaved to the law of matter, and soon fainting under the terrible wheels of the eternal machine which has got out of order.[60]

In our own times there are many practical examples of quasi-Cartesian angelism. For example, "gender ideology," which with Luciferian force has swept through North America and western Europe in the last ten years, rests on the supposition that a person's true "gender" is essentially distinct from the attributes of his body (his reproductive organs and chromosomes), can be known only by the individual through the inspection of his feelings, and demands to be manifested through surgical and hormonal "realignment" of the body with which the individual was born. Poor angel turning the grindstone ... Poor angelistic man mutilating his body, corrupting his mind, and enslaving himself to the incorporeal enemy of the race and nature of man.

DESTROYER OF THE LIFE AND INNOCENCE OF THE CHILD

In the ancient world, and now again in the modern age, the devil wages a war against the life and innocence of the child.

The sin against the child is the sin of this and every century, the sin of the world. From the beginning, the fallen angel, who is proud and will not obey his Creator, has struck out at the child, whose very being signifies humility and the receptivity required for entry to the Kingdom. The Serpent is a perpetual enemy of the Seed of the Woman (cf. Gen 3:15); he wants to kill and devour her Child (cf. Apoc 12:4)—the Divine Child and in him every child. In the ancient world only the Hebrews consistently raised their voices against the slaughter of children. The old religion of Canaan worshipped animals and sacrificed children. In dark groves they offered up the innocent to Moloch. The very name of the Jewish hell, "Gehenna," refers to the vile valley of slaughter, just south of Jerusalem, where children were butchered and burnt to placate "the idols of Canaan" (cf. Ps 105:38;

60   Ibid.

Jer 19:3-6). King David was in no doubt: "the gods of the Gentiles," those false deities who demand the blood of children, "are devils" (Ps 95:5). The words of Hans Urs von Balthasar are hard to refute: "Everywhere outside of Christianity the child is automatically sacrificed." Not every individual pagan is guilty of the hatred of children, but most pagan cultures tolerate the murder of children: if not by cult, then through abortion and infanticide. Reverence for the child is the gift of Christianity, the gift of Jesus Christ, to the world. It is part of the newness that, according to the Church Fathers, the divine Word incarnate brought into human history. And as the modern world turns away from the Virgin and her Child, who makes all things new, so it falls into the old vice of killing its young. The Norwegian Catholic writer Sigrid Undset once wrote: "Where [the Virgin Mother] is driven away, there Herod slinks on his way back and people are seduced by the Idumean's dreams of power and pleasure, of feasts in newly built palaces and blood in dark cellars, and in their hearts Herod's hatred for his own descendants and his fear of children awaken. And the old visions of the goddesses of material change, gods of birth and decay, rising and falling life, again spring up."[61]

THE GREAT EXORCISM:
THE SAVING WORK OF THE WORD MADE FLESH

"For this purpose the Son of God appeared, that He might destroy the works of the devil" (1 Jn 3:8). "Since therefore the children [given to him] share in flesh and blood, he himself likewise partook of the same nature, that through death he might destroy him who has the power of death, that is, the devil, and deliver all those who through fear of death were subject to lifelong bondage" (Heb 2:14). By His Death on the Cross and His Resurrection from

---

61 John Saward, *The Way of the Lamb: The Spirit of the Child and the End of the Age* (Edinburgh: T. & T. Clark, 1999), 3f; quoting Hans Urs von Balthasar, *Das Ganze im Fragment: Aspekte der Geschichtstheologie*, new edition (Einsiedeln: Johannes Verlag, 1990), 282; and Sigrid Undset, "A Christmas Meditation," in *Sigrid Undset on Saints and Sinners* (San Francisco: Ignatius, 1993), 285.

the tomb, the incarnate Son delivers us from the devil, and from his "works," that is, from his evil effects upon us: *sin and death*. Sin came into the world through the first man, Adam, who sinned at the devil's instigation, and through sin death came upon all men, for all men with the first man, their natural head, are like one man and therefore stand and fall together (cf. Rom 5:12).[62] It was the fallen angels who first cast the shadow of death under which we walk in this world, and the scattering of the darkness was the great purpose for which God the Son became incarnate of the Virgin Mary.

> Offending God by his sin, [Adam] drew upon himself the wrath and indignation of God, and consequently death, with which God had threatened him, and together with death captivity in the power of him who henceforth "has the power of death" (cf. Heb 2:14), that is, the devil; and…"the whole Adam, body and soul, was changed for the worse through the offence of his sin" [The Second Council of Orange].[63]

---

62 "All men born of Adam may be considered as one man, inasmuch as they have one common nature, which they receive from their first parents…the multitude of men born of Adam are as so many members of one body" (*ST* 1a2ae q. 81, a. 1). Adam, says Scheeben, "is the natural head of the race precisely because he is the root principle of the entire nature" (*The Mysteries of Christianity*, 365).

63 The Council of Trent, Fifth Session, *Decree on Original Sin* (1546), can. 1; DS 1511. "Mankind is so firmly shackled to the devil that of itself it can in no way recapture the lofty position from which he has cast it down. From this standpoint, man's imprisonment, prescinding from redemption through the God-Man, is absolute and total. But this captivity is nothing else than the culpable privation of the supernatural gifts of the original state, so far as the will of the devil in man's regard is fulfilled in this privation, which man has drawn upon himself by reason of his fellowship with the devil. Accordingly this captivity and the corresponding dominion of the devil over mankind coincide with the mystery of Original Sin itself.… In addition to this, however, experience and revelation teach us that in consequence of the racial guilt God has delivered the race up to a positive dominion of the devil. God permits him in many ways to injure mankind in soul and body, to harm mankind morally and physically, and, in order that man's ambition for self-deification may find its true punishment, to work for that end, that men may adore the devil and his minions instead of the true God. But this dominion of the devil over man does not necessarily mean that man is reduced to full slavery.… For by Original Sin man does not lose his natural as well as his supernatural liberty" (Scheeben, *The Mysteries of Christianity*, 307f).

133

The captivity in which fallen men are held by the devil entails the inability to avoid sin or keep the whole of the natural law without the grace of Christ our Savior, for "he that committeth sin is of the devil" (1 Jn 3:8). The work of man's redemption is therefore a liberation from the devil; it is the first and greatest *exorcism*.

> The Lord Jesus himself described his mission as a reconquest [writes Fr Bonino], an enterprise to extricate man from slavery to Satan, and to bring him back to God. Did he not come to "proclaim release to captives...to set at liberty those who are oppressed" (Lk 4:18)? It is he, "the stronger man," who neutralizes the strong man well-armed, that is, Satan, and strips him of his possessions. *The mission of Jesus appears as a gigantic and salvific exorcism,* a vast clean-up operation, a battle without mercy against the "unclean spirits" who disfigure the image of God: "He went about doing good and healing all that were oppressed by the devil" (Acts 10:38).[64]

From the first day of His public ministry, Jesus casts out the demons, who terrorize men and taunt and attack Him, the Son of Man: "And he was preaching in their synagogues, and in all Galilee, and casting out devils" (Mk 1:39). In His teaching, He reveals to His disciples the corrupting presence and disturbing actions of the demons in the history of the Church and all mankind: "The field is the world. And the good seed are the children of the Kingdom. And the cockle are the children of the wicked one. And the enemy that sowed them is the devil. But the harvest is the end of the world, and the reapers are the angels" (Mt 13:38–39).

In his commentary on St Matthew's Gospel, St Thomas tells us that the cockle, "the children of the wicked one," represents heretics.

> Cockle looks like wheat. So [heretics] pretend and appear to be good, as it says in 1 Timothy 1:7: "Desiring to be teachers of the Law, understanding neither the things they say, nor whereof they affirm."... They were Catholics before they became heretics, for the devil, seeing the Church grow, felt envy, and sowed

---

64 Bonino, 36.

corrupting seed, and moved the hearts of heretics, to do more harm.[65]

The devil's tempting of our Lord in the wilderness is a probing to see if He really is the Son of God, of whose coming in the flesh, as a future event, the devil has long had knowledge.

> As Augustine says, "Christ was known to the demons only so far as he willed: not through anything to do with eternal life, but through temporal effects of his power." From this knowledge they formed a kind of conjecture that Christ was the Son of God. But since they saw in him signs of human weakness, they did not know for sure that he was the Son of God. The devil therefore wanted to tempt him. This is indicated by the words of Matthew when he says that after "he was hungry, the tempter" came "to him" (cf. Mt. 4:2–3), because, as Hilary says, "Had the devil not recognized Christ's humanity in his weakness in feeling hunger, he would not have dared to tempt him." This is also clear in the way the temptation takes place, when the devil says, "If thou be the Son of God." Gregory interprets these words as follows: "What does this way of addressing him mean if not that, though he knew that the Son of God was to come, he did not think he had come in the weakness of the flesh?"[66]

---

65   *Super Matthaeum*, cap 13, lect. 2.
66   *ST* 3a q. 41, a. 1, ad 1. "The rulers of the Jews knew for certain that he was the Christ promised in the Law, which the people did not know. That he was the true Son of God they did not know for certain, but somehow they formed the conjecture that he was. But this conjectural knowledge was obscured in them out of envy and desire for their own glory, which they saw as diminished by the excellence of Christ. The same seems to be true of the wavering of the demons' opinion" (St Thomas Aquinas, *Super 1 Corinthios* cap. 2, lect. 2). "From the beginning, in some way, the angels had knowledge of the mystery of the Kingdom of God, fulfilled by Christ, but that knowledge reached its peak the moment they were made blessed by seeing the Word, a vision the demons never had. Yet even the holy angels did not all know the mystery of the Kingdom perfectly, and to the same degree; much less, then, did the demons have a perfect knowledge of the mystery of the Incarnation when Christ was in the world. As Augustine says, 'it was not made known to them as it was to the holy angels, who enjoy a participation in the eternity of the Word; but it was made known

Throughout His public ministry, and above all in His Passion, our Lord's human opponents show themselves to be vassals of the devil, their "father." They do not believe the truth spoken by Jesus and are therefore offspring of the "father of lies," the once-radiant angel who did not "stand in the truth" (cf. Jn 8:44–45). Satan "enters into Judas" when he goes off to talk with the chief priests about betraying Jesus (cf. Lk 22:4). At the Last Supper the devil puts it into Judas' heart to execute his plan for betraying our Lord (cf. Jn 13:2). The devil does not, *cannot*, force entry into Judas' heart but walks through a door the apostate has left open.[67] When the chief priests and officials of the Temple arrive to arrest our Lord in Gethsemane, He tells them, "This is your hour and the power of darkness" (Lk 22:53). In the human mind of the Son of God, as manifested by His words, the initiator of His Passion and Death is the devil, who deployed the Pharisees and high priests as His instruments. The triumph of the Savior on Good Friday, Holy Saturday, and Easter Sunday was therefore a condemnation and casting out of the diabolical "prince of this world" (cf Jn 12:31), the destruction of the devil and his works (cf. 1 Jn 3:8; Heb 2:14), the disarming and shaming of the fallen principalities and powers (cf. Col 2:14). In our baptism, through water and the Holy Spirit, God the Father applies to our souls the victory of the Lord Jesus: He delivers us "from the dominion of darkness and transfers us to the kingdom of His beloved Son, in whom we have redemption, the forgiveness of sins" (cf. Col 1:13).

"NOT AGAINST FLESH AND BLOOD":
SPIRITUAL BATTLE WITH THE FALLEN ANGELS

Christ our God, crucified and risen, has defeated Satan, but, for our spiritual good, Divine Providence permits the fallen angel in his impotence to taunt and attack us, and to lord it over this

---

by some temporal effects, so as to strike terror into them.' For had they perfectly and certainly known that he was the Son of God, and what the effect of his Passion would be, they would never have procured the crucifixion of the Lord of Glory" (*ST* 1a q. 64, a. 1, ad 4).

67   Cf. the opinion attributed to Titus of Bostra and cited by St Thomas in his *Catena aurea in Lucam*, cap. 22, lect 2.

world, till the great last day when Christ comes again in glory to judge the living and the dead, and the attacks of the evil one will be at an end. St Antony of Egypt tries to instill this truth into his disciples, as an encouragement for their fortitude and a warning for their prudence. "Since our Lord came to live among us, the enemy has fallen, and his powers been enfeebled. So, though he can do nothing, still like a tyrant, he does not bear his fall quietly, but threatens, though the threats are just words. Think about this, and you will be able to despise the demons."[68] Like King Richard III on Bosworth field, the devil is a defeated tyrant; he's finished, and he knows it, and for that very reason is dangerous. Our Lord calls him "the prince of this world," not as if he had a natural and rightful dominion, but because he is a usurper: "Worldly men, despising their true Lord, have made themselves his subjects."[69]

From Pentecost onwards, the Church has been subjected to ceaseless demonic assault, as Christ himself had been; or rather, in every age of the Church's history, the demons strike at the now glorious and invincible Head and Bridegroom by wounding His Mystical Body and Bride. The red dragon with his seven heads and ten horns, the old serpent who is Satan, seeks to devour the sons of Holy Mother Church as soon as they have been re-born by water and the Holy Spirit (cf. Apoc 12:3–4, 9). A great battle is fought in heaven between St Michael with his holy angels and the dragon-devil with his fallen angels; St Michael prevails and throws the devil out of heaven (cf. Apoc 12:7–9). "Heaven" here, argues St Bede, "signifies the Church, in which [John] says that Michael with his angels fights against the devil; he wages war, according to God's will, by praying for the pilgrim Church and supplying her with his help."[70] But Jesus promises that the gates of hell will not prevail against the Church He built on the rock of Peter (cf. Mt 16:18). The disciples receive power from Christ to crush the demonic serpents and scorpions, "and all the power of the enemy," under their feet (cf. Lk 10:17, 19; Rom 16:20).

68 St Athanasius, *Vita S. Antonii*, cap. 28; PG 26.884BC.
69 St Thomas Aquinas, *Super Ioannem* cap. 12, lect. 5.
70 St Bede the Venerable, *Explanatio Apocalypsis* cap. 12; PL 93.167B.

It is the devil who masterminds the persecution of the first Christians (cf. Apoc 2:10) and obstructs the ministry of St Paul (cf. 1 Thess 2:18). Paul says that he and the other apostles are "a spectacle to the world, and to angels and men" (cf. 1 Cor 4:9): "The good angels hastened to comfort them, the evil angels to attack them."[71] The Apostle forgives the Christians of Corinth, in order "to keep Satan from gaining the advantage over us, for we are not ignorant of his designs" (cf. 2 Cor 2:11). If the Apostle were without mercy and unforgiving, he would give an opening to Satan. The devil will use any means he can find to drag men into hell. Moral relativism does the job for him, but so, too, does moralistic rigorism.[72]

If they are to share the exaltation and victory of the divine Head, the members of the Mystical Body must share His humiliations and temptations. In, with, and through Christ, by the merits of His victory over temptation in the wilderness, and by His grace, Christians are called to resist and overcome the tempter. This spiritual combat continues throughout every man's life and the whole of the Church's history. Man's life in this world, as Job learns, is a battle (cf. Job 7:1). St Paul warns us: "Our wrestling is not against flesh and blood; but against Principalities and Powers, against the rulers of the world of this darkness, against the spirits of wickedness in the high places. Therefore, take unto you the armor of God, that you may be able to resist in the evil day, and stand in all things perfect" (Eph 6:12). "Strong in faith," we must resist Satan, the man-eating lion. "Resist the devil, and he will fly from you" (Jas 5:7), because, as St Thomas says, "the more you give into him, the more he gets at you."[73]

According to the Holy Rule of St Benedict, by taking the habit, men and women enlist in a crack regiment posted at the front line of the spiritual battle: they come "to fight for the true King,

---

71 St Thomas Aquinas, *Super 1 ad Corinthios*, cap. 4, lect. 2.
72 "The devil has deceived many, drawing some into committing sins, but others into an excessive rigidity against sinners, so that, if he cannot get them through the perpetrating of misdeeds, he can at least destroy those he already possesses through the harshness of prelates, who, by not correcting them with mercy, lead them into despair, and so destroy them, and the devil has them in his snare" (St Thomas Aquinas, *Super 2 Corinthios* cap. 2, lect 2).
73 *Super Ephesios*, cap. 6, lect. 4.

the Lord Christ, by renouncing [their] own will," and taking up "the supremely strong and glorious arms of obedience."[74] St John Henry Newman speaks for the whole Tradition when he makes this declaration in a sermon: "A fight is the very token of a Christian. He is a soldier of Christ; high or low, he is this and nothing else."[75] The Fathers of the Council of Trent instruct all Christians to pray for the great gift of perseverance, and to take heed lest they fall in the face of a relentless enemy: "Knowing they are reborn unto the hope of glory (cf. 1 Pt 1:3), and not yet unto glory itself, they should be in dread about the battle they must wage with the flesh, the world, and the devil."[76] Those who sin after baptism, say the Council Fathers, "deliver themselves up ... to the devil's power," from which they are liberated through priestly absolution in the sacrament of penance.[77]

St Thomas explains the way in which God's permission of demonic activity serves the glorious and good purposes of His Providence:

> By their nature angels are in the middle between God and men. Now in the plan of Divine Providence the good of lower beings is obtained through higher beings. Divine Providence obtains the good of man in two ways. The first way is direct: we are drawn to the good and away from evil; this is appropriately done by the good angels. The second way is indirect: we are exercised under attack by fighting back against the opposition. It is fitting that this procurement of human good should be supplied by the bad angels, lest after sinning they should cease to be of any use in the order of nature.[78]

---

74 *The Rule of St Benedict,* prologue.

75 St John Henry Cardinal Newman, "God's Will: the End of Life," in *Discourses Addressed to Mixed Congregations,* new edition (London, New York, & Bombay: Longmans, Green, & Company, 1906), 120.

76 The Council of Trent, Sixth Session, *Decree on Justification* (1547), ch. 13; DS 1541. The same Council includes among the effects of extreme unction the grace more easily to resist the devil's temptations; cf. Fourteenth Session, *Doctrine on the Sacrament of Extreme Unction* (1551), ch. 2; DS 1696.

77 The Council of Trent, Fourteenth Session, *Doctrine on the Sacrament of Penance* (1551), ch. 1; DS 1669.

78 *ST* 1a q. 64, a. 4.

Satan is not out of control. He is held in place by God's power, wisdom, and love.[79]

SPIRITUAL BATTLE: THE TRADITIONAL LITURGY

In many ways and on many occasions, the prayers and ceremonies of the traditional liturgy bring home to us the reality of the devil, of the dominion he exercises in this fallen world, and of our spiritual battle with him. In both Christian East and Christian West, exorcism precedes baptism, even of infants. St Thomas explains:

> If you intend to do a job wisely, you first remove the obstacles to the job. As it is written: "Break up anew your fallow ground and sow not upon thorns" (Jer 4:13). Now the devil is the enemy of man's salvation, which man acquires by baptism; and the devil has a certain power over man from the very fact that the latter is subject to original, or even actual, sin. Consequently it is fitting that before baptism the demons should be expelled by exorcisms, lest they impede man's salvation. This expulsion is signified by the [priest] breathing [upon the person to be baptized]; while the blessing, with the imposition of hands, shuts the door against the return of the one expelled. The salt put in the mouth, and the anointing of the nose and ears with spittle, signify the receiving of doctrine as to the ears, approval of doctrine as to the nose, and confession of doctrine as to the mouth. The anointing with oil signifies the person's being equipped to fight against the demons.[80]

---

79 The moral evils perpetrated by His creatures are subject to Divine Providence "as foreknown and ordered (*ordinatum*) by God, but not as intended by Him" (*Sent.* lib. 1, d. 39, q. 2, a. 2).

80 *ST* 3a q. 71, a. 2. In 1975 a *peritus* composed a document on *Christian Faith and Demonology* for the Congregation for the Doctrine of the Faith. Regarding post-conciliar changes to the rite of baptism, the author makes this declaration: "It is true that the ritual for the Christian initiation of adults has been modified on this point. It no longer addresses the devil with words of command. But for the same reason it addresses God in the form of prayers. The tone is less spectacular, but just as expressive and effective. It is therefore wrong to say that exorcisms have been abolished from the new ritual of baptism. Indeed, the extent of the error is clear

In the Sacrament of Confirmation, the baptized Christian is enrolled as a soldier of Christ and receives from the Holy Spirit a special grace to strengthen him for spiritual combat.[81]

In the Ordinary of the traditional Latin Mass, the priest's and every Christian's engagement in spiritual combat is a major theme. At the foot of the altar, in the words of David, the priest asks God to be delivered from "the wicked and deceitful man." In a commentary attributed to St Jerome, the author points out that "no one is more wicked and deceitful than the inventor of wickedness and jealous foe of sanctity, that is, the devil, who entered the heart of Judas for the betrayal of Christ."[82] The priest and the server (on behalf of the people) confess their sins before St Michael, who cast out the devil from the heavens. The holy Gospel is read or sung toward the north, the place of darkness and cold, and therefore a convenient symbol of the evil from which the light of Christ's truth and the fire of His love deliver us. In the "embolism," which follows the *Pater noster*, developing the petition for deliverance from evil (or the evil one), the priest asks for deliverance from "evils past, present, and to come." The future evils are "whatever

---

from the fact that the new ritual of the catechumenate has instituted, before the ordinary, so-called 'major' exorcisms a series of 'minor' exorcisms, which are spread throughout the entire duration of the catechumenate, and which were previously unknown. Thus, exorcisms still remain. Today as yesterday they seek victory over Satan, the devil, the prince of this world, the power of darkness. And the three customary 'scrutinies', in which they have the same place as before, have the same negative and positive purposes as previously, namely, 'to free from sin and from the devil' just as much as 'to make strong in Christ.' The celebration of the baptism of infants also retains, whatever may be said, an exorcism. This in no way means that the Church considers these infants as being possessed, but she does believe that they too need all the effects of Christ's redemption. In fact, before baptism everyone, child or adult, carries the sign of sin and of the influence of Satan" (https://www.vatican.va/roman_curia/congregations/cfaith/documents/rc_con_cfaith_doc_19750626_fede-cristiana-demonologia_en.html). For contrasting thoughts, see Thomas Pink, "Vatican II and Crisis in the Theology of Baptism," in P. Edmund Waldstein, O.Cist., ed., *Integralism and the Common Good*, vol. 2: *The Two Powers* (Brooklyn: Angelico Press, 2022), 290–334.

81 Cf. *ST* 3a q. 71, aa. 1, 4, & 9.

82 *Breviarium in psalmos, Psalmus* 42; PL 28.952A. Cf. St Thomas Aquinas, *Super psalmos* 42, n. 1.

may happen to us through either temptations from the devil or the miseries of the world."[83] As he cleanses the paten over the chalice before consuming the Precious Blood, he unites, in David's words, praise of our Lord with confidence that His Blood will "save him from his enemies," of whom the devil is the chief.

In the traditional prayers of preparation for the celebration of Mass, attributed to St Ambrose, the priest asks our Lord, "High Priest and true Pontiff," to fortify him with "the trusty and devoted care and mighty protection of the blessed angels, that the enemies of all good may depart in confusion," and to "drive away the enemies that seek to ensnare [him]." As he kisses the amice and rests it briefly it on his head before tucking it in around his neck, he prays, "Put the helmet of salvation on my head, O Lord, that I might fight off the devil's attacks." In the prayer to St Michael, one of the Leonine prayers recited after the celebration of Low Mass, we ask the "Prince of the heavenly host" to "cast into hell Satan and all the evil spirits who prowl about the world seeking the ruin of souls."

In the rite of Extreme Unction, the Church displays her awareness that the devil will intensify his attacks when a man is gravely sick or dying, as he did when St Martin of Tours was in his final agony.[84] With his right hand outstretched over the head of the sick person, the priest prays, in the name of the Father, the Son, and the Holy Spirit, that "the whole power of the devil may be extinguished" in him. In the Litany of the Saints, he asks God to deliver him "from the power of the devil." As he commends the soul of the dying man to God, he prays that "foul Satan and his henchmen may give way to [God], and [that], when [God] comes in the company of the angels, [Satan] may tremble, and flee into the deep abyss of unending night."

---

83 Johann Mohren, *Expositio sanctissimae Missae atque rubricarum seu catechismus liturgicus* (Trier: Lintz, 1844), 551.

84 "He saw the devil standing nearby. 'What are you doing here, bloody beast?' he said; 'you will find nothing in me, deadly one. Abraham is taking me into his bosom.' With that he surrendered his spirit up to Heaven" (Sulpicius Severus, *Epistola* 3, Ad Bassulam socrum suam, Quomodo beatus Martinus ex hac vita ad immortalem transierit; PL 20.182D–183A).

"SEEKING WHOM HE MAY DEVOUR":
DEMONIC TEMPTATION

The chief goal of the devil is to induce us to sin and to be obstinate in sin to the end. He ceaselessly prowls around, seeking whom he may devour (cf. 1 Pt 5:8). Temptation is his proper work: St Paul calls him simply "he that tempteth" (1 Thess 3:5). He tempted Christ Himself in the wilderness (cf. Mt. 4: 3–10), incited Judas to betrayal (cf. Jn 13:2, 27), and got Ananias to lie to the Holy Spirit (cf. Acts 5:3). Out of envy the demons want to stop us from reaching the great final good they have lost forever, and out of pride they try to ape the power of God: just as God gives us holy angels to help us, so the devil deputes fallen angels to hinder us. "The ordering of the assault is from God, who knows how to make orderly use of evil by ordering it to the good. As regards the angels, both their guardianship and the ordering of their guardianship are to be referred to God as their first author."[85]

Satan cannot directly influence our intellects or wills, but he can move our lower powers, our external senses, and the internal senses of imagination and memory and in that way, indirectly, can do harm to our thinking and willing. The lower powers are organic and bodily, dependent, for example, upon the health of our brain. Now, as we have seen, angels can affect our bodies, and move bodily things. And so, for example, by means of the pictures he plants in our imagination, the fallen angel can lead our intellects into error, proposing spurious reasons for committing a sin, and he can incline our wills to evil by, for example, arousing passions of the sensitive appetite. He may also fill the soul with despondency and dread by means of "some odious and sickening imagination, in no sense one's own, but forced upon the mind from without."[86] The demons are often busy when we

---

85   St Thomas Aquinas, *ST* 1a q. 114, a. 1.
86   St John Henry Newman speaks of these horrible and unwanted images when looking for an experience in the lives of ordinary men that will shed light on the mental anguish of our Lord in the Garden and on the Cross; cf. "The Mental Sufferings of Our Lord in His Passion," in *Discourses Addressed to Mixed Congregations*, 337.

are asleep and so physically and mentally at our most vulnerable. "The demons imprint shapes and forms on our intellect.... Now it seems to me [writes Evagrios Pontikos] that in our sleep, when the activity of our bodily senses is suspended, it is by arousing the memory that the demons make this imprint."[87]

St Thomas reminds us that, as pure spirits, "the demons do not delight in the obscenities of the flesh, as if they themselves were disposed to carnal pleasures. It is wholly through envy that they take pleasure in all sorts of human sins, so far as they are hindrances to man's good."[88] When the renegade angels tempt men into the grossness of unnatural vice, they turn away with abhorrence, says St Catherine of Siena, from the actual commission of the sin.[89] The devil and his demons will do whatever it takes to cause the eternal loss of a human soul. For some, it will be the sins of the flesh that the fallen spirit by nature finds disgusting, and for others it will be the cold pride that more closely resembles his own wickedness. Those striving with zeal for holiness are unlikely to consent to flagrantly carnal temptations, and so the devil concentrates instead on spiritual seduction, temptations to his own sins of pride and envy, from which he can draw the imprudent man into other depravities. He makes his corrupting suggestions seem noble and beautiful and may even disguise himself as "an angel of light" (cf. 2 Cor 11:14).

> Satan sometimes transforms himself visibly [says St Thomas], as he did in the case of St Martin, to deceive him, and in this way he has deceived many. Now to deal with this danger, the discernment of spirits, which God bestowed in a special way on St Antony, is effective and

---

87 Evagrios the Solitary, "On Discrimination," n. 4; *The Philokalia: The Complete Text Compiled by St Nikodimos of the Holy Mountain and St Makarios of Corinth*, vol. 1 (London: Faber, 1979), 40.

88 *ST* 1a q. 63, a. 2, ad 1.

89 "This sin not only displeases me ... but also the devils whom these wretches have made their masters. Not that the evil displeases them because they like anything good, but because their nature was originally angelic, and their angelic nature causes them to loathe the actual commission of this enormous sin." *The Dialogue of the Seraphic Virgin, Catherine of Siena*, trans. Algar Thorold (London: Burns, Oates, & Washbourne, 1925), 255.

necessary. We can recognize that it is Satan, because, whereas the good angel exhorts us to do good things at the beginning, and then to continue doing them, the evil angel makes a pretense of good things at the beginning, but, wishing to satisfy his own desires and attain what he intends, namely, deception, he leads and goads us into evil things.[90]

We must be vigilant, and not "believe every spirit" (cf. 1 Jn 4:1). The Church does not immediately recognize the authenticity of seemingly angelic visitations, apparent miracles, and claims to private revelations, but, walking the central path of prudence between rationalism and credulity, investigates them through the work of theologians and physicians. The model for her own discernment and prudence is Joshua, who, when he saw the angel in the field, asked: "Art thou one of ours, or of our adversaries?" (Josh 5:13).

Out of whatever evil the fallen spirit does, or tempts men to do, the all-holy Trinitarian God brings good. The devil's power is limited by his created nature, and his actions by the wisdom and love of God. He tempts us not as long us as he likes, but as long as God allows. For a short time, God permits us to be tempted, but eventually He drives away the tempter out of compassion for us in our infirmity.[91] God gives sufficient grace to every man to resist the devil and his demons and allows the intellect and will of no man to be directly attacked. Without Jesus we can do nothing (cf. Jn 15:5), yet with His power strengthening us, we can do anything (cf. Phil 4:13). Through the risen Christ, then, with and in Him and by His grace, we can defeat Satan. All that our divine Head is and does in His human nature is for the benefit of us, His members. It was therefore for us that He conquered Satan, first in His temptations in the wilderness and finally by His Passion and Death on the Cross. The grace by which we conquer the devil when he tempts us was merited by Jesus in these saving mysteries. He is victorious in Himself,

---

90 *Super 2 Corinthios* cap. 11, lect. 3.
91 Cf. *ST* 1a q. 114, a. 5.

and we are victorious through our baptismal incorporation into Him, by His merits, power, and grace. "We are not the doers of these things," says St Antony of Egypt of his exorcisms, "but it is Christ who works them by means of those who believe in him."[92] Temptation proves to us our nothingness as creatures and our vulnerability as the children of Adam; it should therefore be a motive of humility, penitence, and unceasing prayer. *Kyrie eleison!* Attacks are permitted for the final glory of the elect, for it is the Father's will that we should attain eternal glory as a victor's crown.[93]

Indirectly, says St Thomas, the devil is the cause of all human sins, in the sense that the first man sinned at his instigation, and through that sin has come the inclination to sin in all men. "He that committeth sin," says St John, "is of the devil, for the devil sinneth from the beginning" (1 Jn 3:8). Christ's sacrifice of atonement for human sin is therefore the defeat of Satan, as the beloved disciple goes on to say: "For this purpose the Son of God appeared, that he might destroy the works of the devil" (ibid.). The devil is also the cause of all sins in the sense of every kind of sin: there is no sin which the old deceiver does not at some time seduce some human being to commit; nothing is out of bounds for Lucifer. However, not all human sins are the direct result of demonic temptation, for some come from the disorders of our fallen nature, the concupiscence of the flesh or the eyes, or from our pride. St Thomas wants us to keep Satan in his proper proportions. He is not a sovereign principle of evil, as the Manichees thought, but a dangerous fallen creature, who does not and cannot replicate the universal causality of the Infinite and Supreme Good.

The bad angels may not lurk behind all our evil deeds, but the good angels are without doubt involved in all the good we

92   *Vita S. Antonii*, n. 80; PG 26.956A.
93   "There was never a saint so sublimely rapt and enlightened as not to be tempted some time or other. For he is not worthy of the sublime contemplation of God who for God's sake has not been exercised by some tribulation." Thomas à Kempis, *De imitatione Christi*, lib. 2, cap. 9, n. 7 (Mechlin: Dessain, 1921), 104.

do. As St Thomas says: "Man can of his own accord fall into sin: but he cannot advance in merit without the help of God, which is brought to him by the ministry of the angels. Thus the angels cooperate in all our good works, but our sins do not all come from the demons' suggestions."[94] Demons can lead men astray, not by true miracles, but by displays of their superior created angelic power.

> If we take "miracle" in the strict sense, the demons cannot work miracles, nor can any creature, but God alone: since in the strict sense a miracle is something done outside the order of the entire created nature, under which order every created power is contained. But sometimes "miracle" may be taken in a broad sense to mean whatever exceeds human power and experience. In this sense, demons can work miracles, that is, things causing man to be astonished, insofar as they go beyond his power and knowledge. For even a man by doing what is beyond the power and knowledge of another man leads him to be astonished at what he has done, so that in a way he seems to that man to have performed a miracle. Note, however, that, though the works of demons that appear miraculous to us are not real miracles, sometimes they are something real. So, for example, the magicians of Pharaoh by the demons' power produced real serpents and frogs. And "when fire came down from heaven and at one blow consumed Job's servants and sheep; and when the storm struck down his house and with it his children" — these were "the work of Satan, not illusions," as Augustine says.[95]

DEMONIC ATTACKS ON BODIES

Demons can attack bodies as well as souls. As we have seen, the angels possess certain powers over the visible universe, powers the fallen angels retain. They can therefore, according to the masters of sacred doctrine, cause bodily afflictions in human beings and

---

94 *ST* 1a q. 114, a. 3, ad 3.
95 *ST* 1a q. 114, a. 4, citing St Augustine, *De civitate Dei* lib. 20, cap. 19; PL 41.687.

animals, damage to material objects, and disruptions of the weather. Not all such troubles are the knavish tricks of the devil, but any of them could be, and some of them may be. Proof is to be found throughout Scripture. God permits Satan to inflict physical trials on Job (cf. Job 1:12). In the Gospels, our Lord gives speech to a man made dumb by a demon (cf. Mt 10:32), and sight to one blinded by the same agent (cf. Mt 12:22). The poor demoniac living in the tomb has a legion of demons inside him, who at their own request, when cast out, enter a herd of swine (cf. Mk 5:1ff).

The traditional *Rituale romanum* provides many examples of the Church's belief, based on Scripture and Tradition, that the bodily order, good and beautiful though it is as created by God, is subject to demonic interference. There are exorcisms in the *Rituale* of persons possessed or obsessed by demons, but also of salt, water, and oil. Before each is blessed to God's glory and the good of man, it is delivered from the clutches of the devil.

In *The Problem of Pain*, C. S. Lewis argues that many physical evils, apparently without connection with human folly or malice, are to be explained by the activity of fallen angels, who should have been the peaceful administrators of the material world but are now its violent subverters. "It seems to me ... a reasonable supposition, that some mighty created power had already been at work for ill on the material universe, or the solar system, or at least the planet Earth, before ever man came on the scene, and that when man fell, someone had tempted him."[96] Louis Bouyer paints the picture of a visible world shaken and wounded by the pride of a part of the world invisible:

> Something has gone wrong. A fissure has opened in the choir of the first-born spirits. Lucifer, who was sup-posed to be the guardian angel of the cosmos, wanted to make himself its god. With the companions of his infidelity he has crashed into the sensible world.... The beauty of the universe has not entirely vanished. It has become equivocal; it is no longer the pure canticle of intelligent creatures, but the reflection of their conflict,

---

96 *The Problem of Pain* (London: Collins-Fontana, 1957), 122f.

an intersection of light and shadow, a life nourished henceforth on the death to which it tends.[97]

The fact that the devil and his demons have turned away from the vocation given them by God, including their role in the running of the universe, sheds light on the disorders and disasters, seemingly unconnected with human activity, that trouble the physical world. Earthquakes and volcanic eruptions may be manifestations of the natural energies of the earth that the wounded intellects of Adam's sons have not learnt to harness, or they may be disturbances caused by fallen angels conspiring to wreck rather than regulate the functioning of the cosmos.

According to the prophets, apostles, and Church Fathers, the places and objects of pagan worship are inhabited and befouled by demons: "All the gods of the Gentiles are demons," says King David (cf Ps 95:5). This is also the teaching of St Paul: "The things which the heathen sacrifice they sacrifice to demons and not to God" (1 Cor 10:20). It is demons that urge men to turn away from the true God. The devil is not interested in the animals offered to him; his only pleasure, as St Thomas says, is "in being paid the reverence due to God."[98] Only demons, who despise human life and innocence, would demand, as Baal and the deities of Canaan did, the ritual slaughter of children. Their high places and groves were therefore an abomination to the prophets of the true God, the Lord God of Israel.

> It would be temerarious [says Abbot Vonier] to belittle what the early Fathers said of the power of the demons in the pagan temples, in the idols, in the groves and caverns where heathen rites were performed. The demons were loud in their utterances through the mouth of the idols, and many are the incidents in early Church

97 Louis Bouyer, introduction to *Anges et démons: Textes patristiques traduits par Élisabeth de Solms* (Paris: Zodiaque, 1972), 12.
98 *In symbolum apostolorum*, art. 1. The devil says to Jesus: "All these things will I give thee if falling down thou wilt adore me" (Mt 4:9). "The unclean spirits, tied to these images by this wicked art, bring the souls of their worshipers into fellowship with them, and so into a miserable captivity" (St Augustine, *De civitate Dei* lib. 8, cap. 24, n. 2; PL 41.251).

history which prove that the pagan nations were accustomed to exhibitions of unseen powers which could never be considered as powers of light. Then we have, through all the centuries of the Christian spiritual warfare, most authentic records of manifest activities of the demons. The servants of God are persecuted by fierce powers, visibly, physically, in open daylight, as it were.[99]

DEMONIC OBSESSION AND POSSESSION

All men, even the great saints, suffer demonic temptation, as the Lord Jesus did. In some, especially those seriously striving for holiness and a closer loving union with Jesus, the devil's attack may sometimes take the form of *obsession*, that is, the placing of the soul under *siege*. Interiorly, the Christian is troubled by a seemingly fixed idea that exhausts all the energies of his intellect, or by horrible images (phantasms), or, in his emotional life, by feelings of doubt, anger, antipathy, and despair. Demonic obsession can also affect the external senses: the Christian may see apparitions designed to horrify or seduce, hear sounds that frighten or sooth, smell odors foul or sweet. Examples of such attacks can be found in the lives of many saints, such as Antony of Egypt, Catherine of Siena, and the Curé of Ars. Like every evil act of God's creatures, the devil's besieging of a human person is willed by God neither directly nor indirectly but is permitted by Him for the good of purifying and strengthening the soul. In his attacks on the internal senses, the devil may sometimes exploit the natural temperament of the soul under siege: for example, a tendency to scruples or vividness of imagination. However fierce the attack, however relentless and drawn-out the siege, the Christian does not lose his freedom, and with the grace of God, by the power of the holy cross, he can conquer the devil, and the siege will be raised.[100]

The most violent form of demonic attack is possession, in which a demon takes up residence in someone's body, controls

99 Vonier, *Teaching*, 280.
100 Antonio Royo Marín, OP, *Teologia della perfezione Cristiana*, eleventh edition (Milan: San Paolo, 1987), 389–95.

his limbs and senses, and produces effects beyond the person's natural powers or known abilities. The Roman Ritual gives as examples speaking or understanding a foreign language never studied and revealing the secrets of hearts or events in remote places. If obsession is siege, possession is occupation by the enemy. Although the devil cannot enter a man's intellect or directly control his will, he can impede their proper operation. Demonic possession is a physical, not moral evil. It is neither a sin nor in all cases a punishment for sin, though, of course, it may sometimes be, when, for example, someone has opened themselves to invasion by the devil through dabbling in the occult. Great and holy people have suffered possession, such as the Jesuit exorcist of Loudun, Père Surin.[101] We must remember, though, that even in the extremity of possession the devil can do nothing unless God permits it, and that God permits no man to suffer trial, whether from the devil or any other created cause, without giving him the grace to endure. "Not that God will play you false," says St Paul; "He will not allow you to be tempted beyond your powers. With the temptation itself, he will ordain the issue of it, and enable you to hold your own" (Knox, 1 Cor 10:13).

"THE WHOLE ARMOR OF GOD":
HOW WE DEFEAT THE DEVIL

The Church has a supernatural armory for warding off the devil's attacks, and divine remedies for the harm he does. The armor and weapons are the infused virtues of the Christian life, theological and moral; the remedies are the sacraments, prayer, and sacramentals. In the sixth chapter of his epistle to the Ephesians, St Paul makes a checklist of the armaments at our disposal:

> Finally, brethren, be strengthened in the Lord, and in the might of His power. Put you on the armor of God, that you may be able to stand against the deceits of the devil. For our wrestling is not against flesh and blood; but against principalities and powers, against the rulers

---

101   See John Saward, *Perfect Fools: Folly for Christ's Sake in Catholic and Orthodox Spirituality* (Oxford: Oxford University Press, 1980), 124–28.

of the world of this darkness, against the spirits of wickedness in the high places. Therefore, take unto you the
armor of God, that you may be able to resist in the evil
day and to stand in all things perfect. Stand therefore,
having your loins girt about with truth, and having on
the breastplate of justice, and your feet shod with the
preparation of the Gospel of peace. In all things taking
the shield of faith, wherewith you may be able to extin-
guish all the fiery darts of the most wicked one. And
take unto you the helmet of salvation and the sword of
the Spirit (which is the Word of God). (Eph 6:10–17)

The girding of our loins with truth is the real and serious
restraining of our unruly desires through the virtue of temper-
ance.[102] Justice is a breastplate, because, as a breastplate covers the
whole of a man's chest, so justice covers the entire life of virtue:
charity orders all man's virtuous actions toward his supernatural
end, and justice orders the acts of all the virtues toward man's
social end, the common good.[103] Feet shod with the preparation
of the Gospel of peace are Christian minds lifted above everything earthly by the Gospel that proclaims peace to men of good
will.[104] Faith is a shield, because, just as shields repel the arrows
of the opposing army, so faith protects us from the fiery darts of
carnal temptation: "The flesh tempts us by drawing us towards
the passing pleasures of this present life, but our faith shows us
that through those pleasures, if we cling inordinately to them,
we lose the delights of eternal life."[105]

The first and most important of the remedies for the harm the
devil does to us is the devout use of the sacraments: the cleansing
of conscience in the sacrament of penance; the strengthening
of the soul by the grace of Extreme Unction for the devil's final
assaults; and above all, the worthy reception of Holy Communion.
"As a sign of Christ's Passion, by which the demons are conquered,
[the Holy Eucharist] repels all the assaults of demons. And so

102 St Thomas Aquinas, *Super Ephesios*, cap. 6, lect. 4.
103 St Thomas Aquinas, *Super Ephesios*, cap. 6, lect. 4; cf. *ST* 2a2ae q. 58, a. 5.
104 St Thomas Aquinas, *Super Ephesios*, cap. 6, lect. 4.
105 St Thomas Aquinas, *In symbolum apostolorum*, prologus.

Chrysostom says: 'We leave the table like lions breathing fire. We have been made terrible to the devil."[106]

Secondly, prayer is indispensable to the casting out of demons, sometimes accompanied by fasting (cf. Mt 17:20). The holy name of Jesus, when called upon in prayer, has a special power in casting out and warding off the demons: "In my name," says the risen Lord before His Ascension, "they shall cast out devils" (Mk 16:17). To the "pythonical spirit" possessing a girl, St Paul says: "I command thee, in the name of Jesus Christ, to go from her" (Acts 16:18). By their example and teaching, the saints commend the invoking of the holy names of Jesus and Mary in the face of demonic temptation.[107]

Thirdly, the devout use of the sacramentals and other sacred signs: sprinkling holy water[108] and scattering blessed salt, making

---

106 *ST* 3a q. 79, a. 6.

107 "The man engaged in spiritual warfare . . . will see the devil broken and routed by the venerable name of Jesus — will see him and his dissimulation scattered like dust or smoke before the wind." St Hesychios the Priest, "On Watchfulness and Prayer," n. 20; *The Philokalia: The Complete Text Compiled by St Nikodimos of the Holy Mountain and St Makarios of Corinth*, trans. and ed. G. E. H. Palmer, Philip Sherrard, and Kallistos Ware (London: Faber, 1979), 165. "This name of grace/ Gives the melancholic/ A joy angelic/ Banishing every grief you face./ Are you tempted?/ Then invoke this holy name./ From all danger you'll be exempted./ In Mary's name you're sure to find/ Consolation/ For your troubled mind." Cantique 86; *Oeuvres complètes de saint Louis-Marie Grignion de Montfort* (Paris: Seuil, 1966), 1335f.

108 In her autobiography, St Teresa writes: "From long experience I have learnt that there is nothing like holy water to put devils to flight and prevent them from coming back again. They also flee from the cross but return, so holy water must have great virtue. For my own part, whenever I take it, my soul feels a particular and most notable consolation. In fact, it is quite usual for me to be conscious of a refreshment which I cannot possibly describe, resembling an inward joy which comforts my whole soul. This is not fancy, or something which has happened to me only once; it has happened again and again, and I have observed it most attentively. It is, let us say, as if someone very hot and thirsty were to drink from a jug of cold water; he would feel the refreshment throughout his body. I often reflect on the great importance of everything ordained by the Church, and it makes me very happy to find that these words of the Church are so powerful that they impart their power to the water and make it so very different from water which has not been blessed." *The Life of the Holy Mother Teresa of Jesus*, ch. 31, in *The Complete Works of Saint Teresa of Jesus*, trans. and ed. by E. Allison Peers, 1 (London: Sheed & Ward, 1946), 205.

the sign of the cross, wearing the brown scapular and St Benedict medal, and so on. The ruined spirits despise men for their bodiliness, "low-born clods of brute earth," as Newman makes them say,[109] and so it is an exquisite humiliation for them to be driven away by simple material things blessed by a priest.

Fourthly, major or solemn exorcisms for the deliverance of the possessed can be conducted only by priests with authorization from the bishop. Our Lord gave His apostles power over unclean spirits, and after the Ascension, in His name and by His power, they deliver men from Satan's bondage (cf. Acts 5:16; Acts 19:12). This same power is administered by the apostles' successors, the bishops with and under the pope, and is exercised by those to whom they grant the faculty.[110] In her discipline, both of today and in the past, the Church instructs her pastors, when confronted with apparent demonic activity, to discern the spirits by prayer and intelligent reflection, and to avoid the two extremes of rationalistic reductionism and dualistic exaggeration.[111]

After the Holy Eucharist, the greatest of all our God-given helps against the devil is the Mother of God, whose foot crushed the serpent's head (cf. Gen 3:15), and who remains more terrible to him than an army in battle array (cf. Cant 6:10). She is obedience, all Yes to God; he is rebellion, the first to say No to God. She is the Mother of Truth and Fair Love, he the father of lies

---

109 "The Dream of Gerontius," in *Verses on Various Occasions*, 343.
110 "When the Church asks publicly and authoritatively in the name of Jesus Christ that a person or object be protected against the power of the Evil One and withdrawn from his dominion, it is called exorcism. Jesus performed exorcisms and from him the Church has received the power and office of exorcizing. In a simple form, exorcism is performed at the celebration of baptism. The solemn exorcism, called 'a major exorcism,' can be performed only by a priest and with the permission of the bishop. The priest must proceed with prudence, strictly observing the rules established by the Church. Exorcism is directed at the expulsion of demons, or to the liberation from demonic possession, through the spiritual authority which Jesus entrusted to his Church. Illness, especially psychological illness, is a very different matter; treating this is the concern of medical science. Therefore, before an exorcism is performed, it is important to ascertain that one is dealing with the presence of the Evil One, and not an illness" (CCC 1673).
111 The Congregation for the Doctrine of the Faith, *Christian Faith and Demonology* (June 26, 1975). See reference in n. 80 on p. 140.

and the ugliness of hatred. She is thankfulness; he is envy. She is humility; he is pride. St Louis-Marie de Montfort, commending true devotion to the Blessed Virgin, and especially consecration to her, as the surest and most direct way to living union with Jesus, sees her humility as the weapon that strikes fear in the arrogant spirits of hell. "God has made Mary, His holy Mother, the most terrible of the devil's enemies.... Satan, being proud, suffers infinitely more from being vanquished and punished by a little and humble servant of God, and her humility humiliates him more than the power of God does."[112]

Her holy Rosary is a simple but powerful weapon that every soldier of Christ can and should keep in his hands. It defeated the Sultan's fleet at Lepanto, and it can see off Satan when he starts his nonsense. Père Lamy, a Curé d'Ars of the twentieth century, once said: "The recitation of the Rosary, that is what Lucifer hates. He is the declared enemy of the Rosary."[113] A single Hail Mary, said "with attention, devotion, and understanding," is, according to St Louis-Marie de Montfort, "the enemy of the devil, which puts him to flight, the hammer that crushes him, the sanctification of the soul, the joy of the angels, the melody of the predestined."[114]

Finally, the blessed spirits of heaven reinforce us in our combat with the evil spirits of hell. The holy angels not only chant above us in choirs, they also fight for us in regiments. The magnificent hosts of heaven are at war with the marauding powers of hell. St Michael threw Satan out of the heavens when he turned against God, and now he leads the campaign to repulse his attacks on God's servants. Rabanus Maurus — Benedictine bishop, theologian, and poet of the ninth century — praises the great general of the angelic salvation army in his hymn for St Michael's feast:

---

112   *Traité de la vraie devotion à la sainte Vierge* n. 52; *Oeuvres complètes de St Louis-Marie Grignion de Montfort* (Paris: Seuil, 1966), 517f.

113   Comte Paul Biver, *Père Lamy: Apostle and Mystic* (London: Burns, Oates, & Washbourne, 1936), 157.

114   *Traité de la vraie devotion à la sainte Vierge* n. 253; *Oeuvres completes de St Louis-Marie Grignion de Montfort*, 657.

Thee, O Christ, the Father's Splendor,
life and virtue of the heart,
in the presence of the angels
　sing we now with tuneful art,
meetly in alternate chorus
　bearing our responsive part.

Thus we praise with veneration
　all the armies of the sky;
chiefly him, the warrior primate
　of celestial chivalry:
Michael, who in princely virtue
　cast Abaddon from on high.

By whose watchful care, repelling,
　King of everlasting grace!
every ghostly adversary,
　all things evil, all things base;
grant us of thine only goodness
　in thy Paradise a place.[115]

Christ, the glorious God-Man, Mary all fair, and the shining mul-
titudinous legions of the blessed spirits are at our side, guarding
and strengthening us, as we fight off that tiresome minority of
angels who once threw themselves into fire eternal.

A sense of humor is indispensable to the Christian at all times,
but especially when he is fighting the demons. In *Orthodoxy* Ches-
terton suggests that "Satan fell by the force of gravity," because he
took himself seriously to the point of self-worship, whereas "angels
can fly because they can take themselves lightly."[116] Beatrice says

115　Rabanus Maurus, *Hymni* 16, *De S. Michaele archangelo*; PL 112.1659D-
1660A; in *The Monastic Diurnal: or the Day Hours of the Monastic Breviary
in Latin and English* (Farnborough: St Michael's Abbey Press, 2004), 283.
Helen Waddell says of Rabanus: "His faith was absolute, self-condemn-
ing, and passionate: he saw the 'sulphurous stagnant pools' of hell, the
'incense-bearing fields of Paradise,' and the sole hope of men, *Deus immen-
sae bonitatis*, the huge kindliness of God." Referring to his combating of
the double-predestinationism of Gottschalk, she makes this comment:
"He was fighting as best he knew the first menace of the Calvinism that
was later to drive men insane" (*Mediaeval Latin Lyrics* [Harmondsworth:
Penguin, 1952], 321f).
116　*Orthodoxy* (London & New York: John Lane, 1907), 221f.

as much in the passage already quoted from the twenty-ninth canto of the *Paradiso*:

> The prime cause of the fall was the accursed
>   pride of the angel whom you saw beneath
>   all the weight of the cosmos, crushed and pressed;
>
> But these kept humble tenor, knew themselves
>   as rising from the generosity (*bontate*)
>   that made them quick to understand so much,
>
> So were their eyes exalted, raised thus high
>   by merit and illuminating grace,
>   and now their will is firm and full and free.[117]

Succumbing to Satan's attack, Adam fell into something similar to his grim gravity. Cast out of Eden, "by his own fault, he took up grief and toil,/ pawning his honest laughter and sweet play."[118]

St Antony of Egypt laughed at Satan's pretensions and impotence:

> We, the faithful, must not be afraid when he appears, or give heed to his words; he is a liar, and there is not a grain of truth in what he says. He may boldly utter many grand words, but the reality is that he has been drawn by the Savior with a hook like a dragon, and as a beast of burden had a halter tied round his nostrils, his nostrils bound with a ring as a fugitive, and his lips pierced with a band. He was bound by the Lord as a sparrow, *that we should mock him.*[119]

The devil is real and dangerous, yet also ridiculous and desperate, and so not to be feared by those with living faith in God Incarnate, the conqueror of hell. Beatrice had the right attitude. She was *smiling* when she spoke to Dante of the fall of the angels.

---

117   *Paradiso* 29, 55–63; Esolen, 312–13.
118   *Purgatorio* 28, 94–96; Esolen, 307.
119   St Athanasius, *Vita Antonii* n. 24; PG 26.880A. "The proud spirit cannot endure to be mocked" (St Thomas More, *The Dialogue of Comfort against Tribulation*, ed. Monica Stevens [London: Sheed & Ward, 1973], 126).

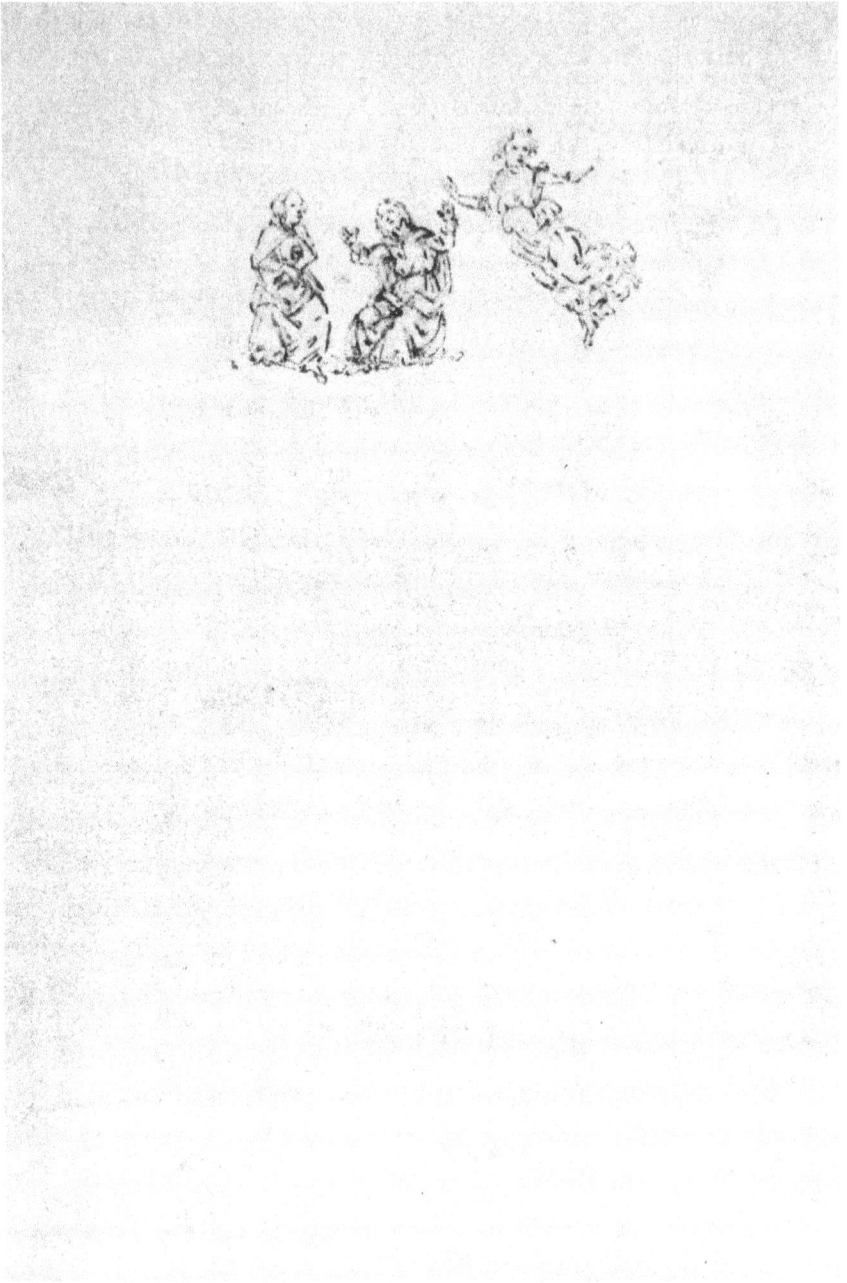

BOTTICELLI, PARADISO 32

5

SINGING · "AVE · MARIA"

THE ANGELS AND THEIR QUEEN

Virgin and Mother, daughter of your Son,
   humbler and loftier past creation's measure,
   the fulcrum of the everlasting plan,

You are she who ennobled human nature
   so highly that its Maker did not scorn
   to make Himself His own creature.[1]

AR ABOVE THE HIGHEST CIRCLE OF the angels, the ever-virgin Mother of God, *daughter of her Son*, sits enthroned at His side. St Bernard of Clairvaux, "the last of the Fathers," leads Dante to her, bidding him to "that face which most resembles Christ/ Lift up [his] gaze," for "its radiance alone/ Can grant to [him] the power to look on Christ."[2] The poet raises his eyes to Our Lady, and she looks down on him, but then straightaway directs him toward the higher beauty, the eternal light of the Triune God, which she sees more clearly and closely than any other created person does, angel or man: "No eye of living creature could aspire/ To penetrate so fixedly therein." In the perfection of her vision of God, and in the nobility of her person, the humble handmaid of the Lord is raised above all other creatures, and is thus Queen of heaven and earth, of the men whom she cherishes as her children, and of the angels who serve her as soldiers. In his sketch of the

---

1 *Paradiso* 33, 1–6; Esolen, 350–51.
2 *Paradiso* 32, 85–87; Sayers-Reynolds, 336. Dom Mabillon says of St Bernard that he is "the last of the Fathers, but certainly not unequal with the first" (Jean Mabillon, OSB, *S. Bernardi opera, praefatio generalis*, n. 23; PL 182.25–26).

penultimate canto of the *Paradiso*, Botticelli shows the Virgin
Mother in the far distance with her divine Son on her left. He
is holding up His hands to display the marks of the nails in the
palms. St Gabriel hovers above Him on His left. At the very end
of the *Commedia*, Botticelli, in keeping with Dante's intentions,
reminds us of the Son of God's becoming flesh of Mary's flesh,
and of His sufferings and glorification in the flesh, which are the
mysteries that open up Paradise and fellowship with the angels
for the poor banished children of Eve. Gabriel, archangel of the
Annunciation, represents all nine orders of the blessed spirits in
the worship of God incarnate, the Redeemer of man, and the
service of His ever-virgin Mother.[3]

MOTHER OF THE CREATOR, QUEEN OF EVERY CREATURE

The first reason for the Blessed Virgin's queenship, indeed the
reason for all her privileges and graces, is her divine motherhood,
a dignity beyond anything attained or attainable by other creatures: "The humanity of Christ [says St Thomas] because it is
united to God, created happiness because it is the enjoyment of
God, and the Blessed Virgin because she is the Mother of God,
have a kind of infinite dignity through the infinite good that is
God. So there cannot be anything better than these, just as there
cannot be anything better than God."[4]

The dignity of being Mother of God is not infinite in an
unqualified sense, since the subject of the relation is a creature
and therefore finite of her very nature. However, it is infinite
in a certain respect, because of the divine and therefore infinite
person of whom the Blessed Virgin is Mother. According to the
theologians of the Schools, the dignity of divine motherhood
pertains to the "hypostatic order." It is a dignity concerning the
very person or hypostasis of Our Lady, not just the function
she performs or the supernatural endowments of her nature.
Divine motherhood, relating the lowly handmaid of the Lord to

---

3   Illustration of Canto 32 of the *Paradiso* (no page number) in Kenneth
Clark, *The Drawings by Sandro Botticelli for Dante's* Divine Comedy.
4   *ST* 1a q. 25, a. 6, ad 4.

the Second Person of the Blessed Trinity, surpasses by far her privileges in grace and glory, her Immaculate Conception and Assumption. It is because she is the Mother of God that she is conceived immaculate and assumed bodily into heaven.[5] It is likewise because she is the Mother of God, the King of Kings, that Mary is Queen. The kingship of the Son redounds to the honor of the mother.

> Christians [says Pope Pius XII] have always believed, and not without reason, that she of whom was born the Son of the Most High, who "will reign in the house of Jacob forever," the Prince of Peace, King of Kings, and Lord of Lords, received privileges of grace above every other creature of God.... And when Christians considered the intimate bond between Mother and Son, they readily acknowledged the royal excellence of the Mother of God.... She bore a Son who, at the very moment of his conception, because of the hypostatic union of the human nature with the Word, was even as man King and Lord of all. So, rightly and justly, St John Damascene could write: "When she became Mother of the Creator, she truly became Queen of every creature."[6]

The Church's hymns, in both West and East, praise Mary as the Queen of Heaven. The Latin Church sings the *Ave regina caelorum* and *Regina caeli* during Lent and Eastertide and the *Salve regina* after Trinity Sunday and throughout the year with the Rosary. The faithful of the Byzantine rite commemorate the Queenship of the Theotokos even more frequently. At every celebration of the Liturgy of St John Chrysostom, the priest places part of the unconsecrated host, representing the Mother of God,

---

5   "The Divine Motherhood is a dignity that by reason of its term, namely, by reason of the person of the incarnate Word, pertains to the hypostatic order, which surpasses the order of grace and glory." Reginald Garrigou-Lagrange, OP, *Mariologia*, art. 1, in *De Christo Salvatore: Commentarius in IIIam partem* Summae theologicae *sancti Thomae* (Turin & Rome: Marietti, 1949), 504.

6   Pope Pius XII, Encyclical Letter *Ad caeli reginam* (October 11, 1954); AAS 21 (1954), 627 & 633.

on the right side of the main part, which symbolizes the Lamb of God, and, as he does so, he repeats the words of the psalm of Mary's Queenship, "The queen stood on thy right hand, in gilded clothing" (Ps 44:10). On many other days, the Greek Church calls upon the Mother of God as *vasilissa*, Queen (or better, Empress) of God's people. In every case, the Queenship of the Mother is connected with the divinity and kingship of the Son: "Adorned in a garment of gold, the Queen is now beside her Son, the King. Beyond all compare more exalted is she than the angels who cry out: 'Glory be to thy power, O Christ.'"[7]

Our Lady is queen by analogy, not with absolute monarchs like Elizabeth Tudor and Catherine the Great, but with those women whose royalty is relative to someone else, a husband or son. Under the Old Law, it was the King's mother, not his consort, who was "the Great Lady" (*gebîrah*).[8] The same is true of the New Law. Like earthly queens, the Blessed Virgin rules her spiritual subjects principally through her union in glory with her Son, the divine King, and through her intercession for His subjects and hers. To serve God is to reign.[9] Now no creature has served God with greater purity, humility, and love than His lowly Handmaid and Mother. Therefore, she reigns above all other creatures, the Queen of heaven and earth, of angels and of men.

In his encyclical on Our Lady's queenship, Pope Pius XII quotes Leo XIII, who said that an "almost immeasurable" power has been given to Mary in the distribution of graces. This power she exercises, added St Pius X, "as by the right of a mother," because she is the Mother of God and, by His gift, Mother of men. Pius XII concludes: "Let all Christ's faithful glory in being subjects of the Virgin Mother of God, who, while enjoying royal power, is

---

7   Cited by Joseph Ledit, *Marie dans la liturgie de Byzance* (Paris: Beauchesne, 1976), 243.

8   See Roland de Vaux, OP, *Ancient Israel: Its Life and Institutions* (London: Darton, Longman & Todd, 1961), 117f.

9   "O God, whom to know is to live, whom to serve is to reign" (Postcommunion of the Votive Mass for Peace, *Missale romanum* 1962; cf. St Gregory the Great, *Missa pro pace, Liber sacramentorum* [PL 78.206A]).

on fire with motherly love."[10] Our Lady, said St Thérèse with the insight of a Doctor of the Church, is "more Mother than Queen."[11]

St Anselm proclaims his confidence in the power of Mary, our Queen and Mother, to help us:

> We have Apostles, Patriarchs, Prophets, Martyrs, Confessors, and Virgins: they are good, very good helpers. But you, O Lady, are better and more exalted than all of these, because you are the sovereign holding sway over these and all other holy ones, even the angelic spirits, as well as the kings and mighty ones of this world, rich and poor, masters and servants, great and small, and what they can do with you, you alone can do without any of them. Why can you do this? Because you are the Mother of our Savior, the Bride of God, the Queen of heaven and earth and all the elements within them. To you, therefore, do I reach out, to you do I fly, and I humbly beseech you to help me in all things. When you are silent, no one prays, no one can help. But when you pray, all pray, and all can help.[12]

"MORE GLORIOUS THAN THE SERAPHIM": MARY, QUEEN OF ANGELS

> And in that center, with their wings outspread,
>   I saw more than a thousand angels in festival,
>   each distinct in radiance and in art.
>
> There, on their play and on their song,
>   I saw a beauty smiling that gave gladness
>   to the eyes of all the other holy ones.[13]

---

10 Pope Pius XII, *Ad caeli reginam*, 637.

11 "Of course, the Blessed Virgin is Queen of heaven and earth, but she is more Mother than Queen, and we must not say that because of her privileges she eclipses the glory of all the saints, as the sun on its rising makes the stars disappear. *Mon Dieu!* How strange that would be! A Mother who made the glory of her children disappear" (The *Carnet jaune* of Mother Agnès, conversation of August 21, 1897, in St Thérèse of Lisieux, *Oeuvres complètes: Textes et dernières paroles*, ed. Jacques Longchampt [Paris: Cerf, 1992], 1103).

12 *Oratio 46, ad sanctam Mariam Virginem*; PL 158.944A.

13 *Paradiso* 31, 130–35; author's translation.

The beauty that smiles on the angels, that causes them joy, is the beauty of Mary, their Queen. Our Lady is Queen of heaven and earth because she is the Mother of the Creator and King of heaven and earth, and for the same reason she is Queen of the Angels, for the angels are the first creatures to inhabit heaven. In his exposition of Psalm 44, St Thomas says that the Blessed Virgin stands in heaven "above all the choirs 'in gilded clothing,' that is, gilded with divinity, not that she is God, but because she is the Mother of God."[14] Above all the choirs of the invisible world of the angels and the myriad galaxies of the visible cosmos is the humble Jewish maiden of the house of David chosen to be Mother of the Creator and Queen of all He has made, the Queen of the universe. "Glorious things of thee are spoken, O Mary, who art this day exalted high above the choirs of angels."[15]

In his conferences on the *Ave Maria*, preached not long before his death, St Thomas shows with more detailed argument how, as Mother of God, Blessed Mary Ever-Virgin surpasses the angels:

> She outshines the angels in familiarity with God. The angel indicated this when he said, "The Lord is with thee," as if to say, "I show thee reverence, for thou art more familiar with God than I am...." *The Lord*, he says, *the Father with the same Son is with thee*, an intimacy no angel or any creature enjoys, for "the holy which shall be born of thee shall be called the Son of God" (Lk 1:35).... *The Lord, the Son*, is in her womb. "Rejoice and praise, O thou habitation of Zion, for great is He that is in the midst of thee, the Holy One of Israel" (Is 12:6).... The Lord is with the Blessed Virgin differently than He is with the angel, for He is with her as Son, but with the angel as Lord. *The Lord, the Holy Spirit*, is with her, as in a temple, which is why she is called "the temple of the Lord, the sanctuary of the Holy Spirit," for she conceived by the Holy Spirit. "The Spirit of the Most High will come upon you." Thus, the

---

14   St Thomas Aquinas, *Super psalmos* 44, n. 7.
15   *Gloriosa dicta sunt de te, Maria, quae hodie exaltata es super choros angelorum* (Introit of the Mass of the Vigil of the Assumption [1962 missal]).

Blessed Virgin has greater familiarity with God than the angel has, because with her is *the Lord Father, the Lord Son, and the Lord Holy Spirit*, that is, the whole Trinity is with her. Thus, it is sung of her, *Totius Trinitatis nobile triclinium*, "noble resting-place of the whole Trinity."[16]

St Thomas questions the orthodoxy of those who imagine that man is so inferior to the angels that in heaven glorified human souls constitute a tenth order below the nine of the angels: "This position is contrary to the sayings of the Fathers, and seems to savor of heresy, since the Blessed Virgin is exalted above the choirs of angels."[17] Fr Bonino comments:

> We must distinguish between the natural hierarchy of beings, which is immutable, and the supernatural hierarchy based on the degree of participation in grace and glory. Grace and glory are given to the angels as a function of their place in the natural hierarchy, and so a higher angel always receive a greater grace. By contrast, grace and glory are given to men as a function of the good pleasure of God alone. It follows that a human creature can obtain a degree of supernatural glory equal or superior to that of the angels. Thus, in virtue of the grace of union, the humanity of Christ, his very body, is exalted above purely spiritual creatures. Likewise, the Virgin Mary has been filled from the outset with the highest grace a creature could receive, for she is the Mother of God, which places her in the order of sanctity above the angels.[18]

This truth is proclaimed at every celebration of the Liturgy of St John Chrysostom, shortly after the Consecration: "Greater in honor than the Cherubim and beyond compare more glorious than the Seraphim, without corruption you gave birth to God the Word; truly the Mother of God, we magnify you."[19] Writing in the fourth century, St Ephrem, Syrian Deacon-Doctor of the Church, makes

---

16 *Super* Ave Maria, a. 1.
17 *Sent.* lib. 2, d. 9, q. 1, a. 8.
18 Bonino, 235.
19 *Divine Liturgy*, 35.

the same point and in similar words: "Beyond compare greater than the Cherubim and Seraphim, and far more glorious: the splendor of the angels, protection of men, key to the door to heaven."[20]

THE KNEELING ARCHANGEL

In many sacred images of the Annunciation, the angel Gabriel *kneels* when he brings the news that the Virgin of Nazareth is to conceive and give birth in the flesh to the Son of the Most High. He recognizes that he is a servant in the presence of a sovereign; the Mother of God is a greater person than he, nearer to God than he. Thereafter, as Dante in the company of St Bernard sees for himself, in the glory of heaven St Gabriel honors with chivalrous devotion the humble Virgin for whose service he was created:

> The angel who first thither made descent,
> > Before her, sang, *Hail Mary, full of grace,*
> > His wings spread wide unto their full extent.

> Response to that divine canticle of praise
> > Was sung by all that court so blissfully
> > still more serenely joyful was each face.

The poet asks the holy abbot of Clairvaux to tell him who the angel is that "looks in our Lady's eyes with love so burning/ That like a fire he seems, so radiant bright."

> "All joy and excellence that dwell," he said,
> > "In soul or angel (and 'tis rightly so)
> > In him is at its most sublime displayed;

> For this is he who brought the palm below
> > To Mary when the Son of God on high
> > Bearing our fleshly burden willed to go."[21]

St Thomas tells us there are three reasons it was appropriate for an *angel* to "bring the palm" to Mary, that is, to announce the mystery of the Incarnation of the Son of God:

---

20   *Oratio ad Deiparam; Ephraem Syri opera omnia,* vol. 3, ed. G. S. Assemani (Rome: 1743), 528f.
21   *Paradiso* 32, 94–99, 103–14; Sayers-Reynolds, 336–37.

First, it preserves the order established by God, by which divine things are brought to human beings by means of angels.... Secondly, it was appropriate for the restoration of human nature that was to come through Christ. As Bede says in a homily: "It was a suitable beginning for man's restoration that God should send an angel to the Virgin to consecrate her by the divine birth, since the first cause of man's ruin was through the devil sending the serpent to deceive the woman by the spirit of pride." Thirdly, it was in harmony with the virginity of the Mother of God. As [Pseudo-]Jerome says in a sermon on the Assumption: "It is good that an angel be sent to the Virgin; because virginity is always akin to the angels. To live in the flesh and not according to the flesh is not an earthly but a heavenly life."[22]

St Thomas notes the different ways in which Zechariah and Mary respond to the angel. The father of the Baptist is troubled by *seeing* the angel (cf. Lk 1:12), but the Mother of God by *hearing* what the angel has to say (cf. v. 29). "The Blessed Virgin was used to visions of angels, and so was disturbed not by seeing the angel, but with wonder at hearing what the angel said to her, for she did not think so highly of herself. So the Evangelist does not say she was troubled at the sight of the angel, but 'at his saying.'"[23]

There is no redemption of the fallen angels, but, according to St Bernard, there is need for a restoration of the heavenly order disturbed by their defection, and in this restoration Mary of Nazareth, Queen of Angels, has a part to play: "[The angel Gabriel] comes to the chosen Virgin of the King, and with special haste, so that, since the angels had a King, they might also have a queen. To make good the ruining of the angelic orders, sinners enter upon the way to Paradise, the Mother of Mercy and Queen of Angels becomes the gate of heaven."[24]

---

22 *ST* 3a q. 30, a. 2.
23 *ST* 3a q. 30, a. 3, ad 3.
24 St Bernard of Clairvaux, *Tractatus ad laudem gloriosae Virginis Matris*; PL 182.1142B. See 110 above.

QUEEN OF VIRGINS, QUEEN OF ANGELS

Our Lady is Virgin of Virgins, Queen of Virgins, and in this respect, too, she has a glory greater than that of the angels. Mary's virginity is fruitful, says St Francis de Sales, while the virginity of the pure spirits is barren. Our Lady gave birth in the flesh to the Son of God, who is the "sweet Fruit of Life, our Lord and Master," and she is the spiritual mother to many other virgins, for, says St Francis, it is "in imitation of her . . . that virgins have vowed their virginity." Thirdly, the virginity of the Mother of God has the power to convert and transform. Mary Immaculate, holier and therefore humbler than all, is ready to share her purity with the impure:

> The purity and virginity of our Lady had this excellence, this privilege, and this supereminence above the virginity of the angels: it was a fruitful virginity. The virginity of the angels is sterile and can have no fruitfulness. The virginity of our glorious Mistress, by contrast, not only was fruitful in bringing forth the sweet fruit of life, our Lord and Master, but also gave birth to a good number of virgins. In imitation of her, virgins have vowed their chastity, but the virginity of this divine Mother has also the property of re-establishing and restoring those who have been soiled and stained at some time in their life.[25]

Finally, says St Francis, our Lady's virginity is superior to the angels' because it is chosen, vowed, and sustained forever, even in her marriage with her spouse most chaste, whereas the angels' virginity is part of their nature as bodiless spirits. Angelic virginity is just a fact about them, but Mary's virginity is freely vowed and the outward expression in her body of the dedication of her mind and heart to her divine Son.

---

25 *Sermon de profession pour la fête de l'Annonciation,* March 25, 1621; *Oeuvres de Saint François de Sales, évêque et prince de Genève et docteur de l'Église,* vol. 10 (Annecy: J. Niérat, 1898), 51.

MOTHER OF DIVINE GRACE, QUEEN OF ANGELS

Our Lady surpasses the angels in grace. Her fullness of sanctifying grace is proportionate to her dignity as Mother of God. But as Mother of God she surpasses in dignity all creatures, including the highest of the Seraphim. Therefore, in grace, too, she is placed far above the angels. The grace the angels received in their first state cannot be compared with that of Mary, nor with the glory she now enjoys, for glory is but the consummation of grace.

Are the angels in any way *indebted* to Our Lady in the supernatural order? Not directly, but indirectly, through her spiritual mothering of men, for the Mother of God is the Mediatrix of all the graces by which Adam's sons are redeemed.[26] As a creature she cannot be ranked with the One who is both her Child and her Creator, yet by His grace, through her faith and love, she cooperated on earth with Him in the meriting of man's salvation, and now, in beatific vision and with beatific love, she cooperates in applying His saving work to the individual souls of men. The Blessed Virgin is the "aqueduct," as St Bernard puts it, that conveys the living waters of the Holy Spirit to our souls.[27] The grace by which a sinner repents comes to him from the Trinitarian Godhead as principal cause, through the Precious Blood of the Lamb as an instrumental cause united to the Godhead, and through the motherly intercession of our Lady as an instrument separate from God. But such repentance brings joy to the holy angels (cf. Lk 15:10), who delight in God's saving will. Therefore, for angels as well as men, Mary is the "cause of joy." There are supernatural blessings, accidental joys, bestowed upon the angels through the mediation of Mary.

---

26   Our Lady is "the dispenser of all the gifts Jesus obtained for us by his Death and his Blood": St Pius X, Encyclical Letter *Ad diem illum* (February 2, 1904); DS 3370. Our Lord chose to make his Mother "the advocate of sinners and the servant and Mediatrix of grace" (Pope Pius XI, Encyclical Letter *Miserentissimus redemptor* [May 8, 1928]; AAS 20 [1928], 178).

27   *In nativitate B. V. Mariae sermo 1, De aquaeductu*, nn. 3–5; PL 183.440AD.

CRUSHING THE SERPENT'S HEAD:
QUEEN OF ANGELS BY CONQUEST

Our Lady is Queen by conquest as well as by relationship; she shares with her Son in His victory over His and our enemies, the fallen angels. This queenly victory is prophesied by the first announcement of the Gospel in Genesis: "I will put enmities between thee [the Serpent] and the woman, and thy seed and her seed. She shall crush thy head, and thou shalt lie in wait for her heel" (Gen 3:15). Blessed Mary acquired dominion over her subjects not only by *being* Mother of the divine King, but also by *cooperating* with Him in His kingly work of redemption. This cooperation began with her consent to His assumption of human nature in her womb, reached its finest hour at the foot of the cross, and continues through the ages of ages in the glory of heaven. First, by faith and love on Calvary, she united herself to our Lord's meriting of the graces the sons of Adam need to be saved; then, in blessed vision and by loving intercession in heaven, she serves our divine Redeemer and King in the distribution of His graces.

In her Immaculate Conception and her bodily Assumption, Blessed Mary ever-virgin receives in a most perfect way the fruits of her Son's defeat of Satan, and in both mysteries shares His triumph. From the first moment of her conception, she was preserved from all stain of original sin, and so, by the anticipated power of her Son's saving merits, from the very beginning of her existence, and forever, she has enmity with the Serpent.[28] Human

---

28 "It was wholly fitting that so wonderful a mother should be ever resplendent with the glory of most sublime holiness and so completely free from all taint of original sin that she would triumph utterly over the ancient serpent.... [The Fathers and ecclesiastical writers] ... taught that by this divine prophecy the merciful Redeemer of mankind, Jesus Christ, the only begotten Son of God, was clearly foretold: that his most Blessed Mother, the Virgin Mary, was prophetically indicated; and, at the same time, the very enmity of both against the Evil One was significantly expressed. Hence, just as Christ, the Mediator between God and man, assumed human nature, blotted the handwriting of the decree that stood against us, and fastened it triumphantly to the cross, so the Most Holy Virgin, united with him by a most intimate and indissoluble bond, was, with him and through him, eternally at enmity with the evil Serpent, and

beings conceived in original sin are placed, till baptismal grace delivers them, in a certain captivity under Satan, but our Lady, conceived immaculate, never comes under his sway: she comes into being crushing his head. Likewise, in her bodily Assumption, she conquers Satan, for it is by his envy, through the sin that Adam committed at his instigation, that death came into the world; the devil is the emperor of death (cf. Heb 2:14), and the despiser of bodily life. As Pope Pius XII said when he defined the dogma of the Assumption:

> Since the second century, the holy Fathers have pre-sented the Virgin Mary as the New Eve. Though subject to the New Adam, she is most closely associated with him, as the protoevangelium foretold (cf. Gen 3:15), in his struggle against the infernal foe. The outcome of the struggle was total victory over sin and death, which the Apostle of the Gentiles always mentions together in his writings (cf. Rom. ch. 5 & 6; 1 Cor. 15:21–26, 54–57). Consequently, just as the glorious Resurrection of Christ was an essential part and the final trophy of this victory, so the struggle common to the Blessed Virgin and her Son was concluded by the glorification of her virginal body, for the same Apostle says: "When this mortal thing hath put on immortality, then shall come to pass the saying that is written: Death is swal-lowed up in victory."[29]

It is fitting, then, that, in the Apocalypse, the Apostle John describes St Michael's defeat of Satan just after he has mentioned the Woman and her Child (cf. Apoc 12:7ff). In the mysteries of man's redemption, Our Lady is triumphant with the holy angels

---

most completely triumphed over him, and thus crushed his head with her immaculate foot" (Pope Pius IX, *Ineffabilis Deus*). If she, the Woman, crushes the head of the Serpent, then he has no power over her in any respect, or at any time. But one of the consequences of Original Sin is being under the power of the devil (cf. Trent, *Decree on Justification*, ch. 1; DS 1521). Therefore, the Blessed Virgin, from the first moment of her existence, is free from Original Sin.

29 Pope Pius XII, Apostolic Constitution *Munificentissimus Deus* (November 1, 1950); AAS 17 (1950), 768.

and over the fallen ones. In soul and body, the humble Virgin sums up all the beauty of a universe recreated in her Son, the eternal Word made flesh.

> For us you are the torch of the noonday
> of charity; below you are the spring
> of ever-living hope for men that die....

> In you is mercy, in you is piety,
> in you magnificence, in you the sum
> of excellence in all things that come to be.[30]

---

30   *Paradiso* 33, 13–15, 19–21; Esolen, 350–51.

ANGELS·AT·THE·END

O Light eternal, dwelling within yourself alone,
  you know yourself, and, known by yourself
  and knowing, you love and smile.

The circle conceived in you
  appeared within you like a reflected light,
  when surveyed somewhat by my eyes,

Within itself, and in its own color,
  it seemed to me painted with our human likeness,
  and with it my gaze was all absorbed.

Like the geometer set on
  squaring the circle, who, for all his thinking,
  doesn't find the principle he needs,

So was I at this new sight:
  I wanted to see how the image
  fits the circle and takes its place there;

But for that my feathers were insufficient,
  save that my mind was struck
  by a flash in which also came desire.

Here my high fantasy failed in power;
  already my longing and my willing
  were turned, like a wheel in equal motion,

By the Love that moves the sun and the other stars.[1]

DANTE HAS REACHED THE SUMMIT OF his endeavor. The Queen of Angels, St Bernard, and Beatrice have brought him to the near presence of the Blessed Trinity. Within the *light eternal* of the Godhead, in some way[2] he sees God *knowing* and God *known*, the Father and

---

1 *Paradiso* 33, 124–45; author's translation.
2 The precise way in which Dante *sees* God at the conclusion of the *Paradiso* is discussed by Kenelm Foster, OP, *The Two Dantes and Other Studies*, 66–85.

His Word (the Son), and the *Love*, the Holy Spirit, by whom the Father and the Son love each other, and in whom They *smile* upon each other and upon the world. In the person of the Son, *the circle conceived in* the Father, he recognizes *our likeness in its proper color*; that is, our humanity in its undiminished integrity. The poet by his natural powers cannot understand how the hypostatic union of human nature with the Word can be *squared* with the immutability and simplicity of God. But the *Light eternal* strikes his mind with a sudden flash, and his will is stirred with longing by the Love that creates all things, the visible universe of bodies and the *world invisible* of the bodiless powers. Dante ends his *Comedy* where all things end in the cosmos, with *the Love that moves the sun and the other stars*. Stars and starfish, Seraphim and sons of men: the Triune God brings them into being and sustains them in being, and moves them, draws them, each to its proper fulfilment and so to Himself, the Supreme Good who is the end of all things.[3] As for man, his final flourishing is a supernatural end: the glorification of his soul in the face-to-face vision of God, which the incarnate Son merited for him in His Passion,[4] and the overflow of glory from his soul into his body in the general resurrection,[5] of which the Son's own Resurrection in the flesh is the instrumental and exemplary cause.[6]

The holy angels, beholding the face of the Father in heaven, already rest at peace in their end, but those among them who also have a ministry on earth work without ceasing to bring human beings to the same glorious goal. As the holy angels serve the Triune God of Love by their supervision of the movements of *the sun and the other stars*, so they serve Him by their guardianship in the movement of each man toward his last breath and particular judgement, and of all mankind toward the last great day of general resurrection and judgement.

---

3 Cf. *SCG* lib. 3, cap. 17 & cap.18.
4 Cf. *ST* 3a q. 48, a. 1.
5 Cf. *ST* 3a q. 28, a. 2, ad 3.
6 Cf. *ST* 3a q. 56, a. 1, ad 3.

GO FORTH, O CHRISTIAN SOUL!

The angels will be with us at the end. In many of the prayers of the Church's traditional last rites, the priest calls upon the holy angels to assist the dying Christian. Before administering Extreme Unction, the priest asks the Lord Jesus Christ to drive away the fallen angels and all malevolent discord, and to comfort the dying with the presence of the angels of peace. He bids the Christian soul "go forth" (*proficiscere*) in the name of the three divine Persons, of the Mother of God, of St Joseph, and of the blessed spirits in their ninefold glory: "May your place be this day in peace and your dwelling in holy Zion." The priest goes on to say in a second prayer of commendation: "May Satan and his minions be frightened into making way for you, and when you arrive in the company of angels, may he tremble and flee into the monstrous chaos of eternal night."

Our guardian angels' great work is to get us to heaven. What happens, if, by God's mercy, we finally arrive there? St John Henry Newman provides a hint in *The Dream of Gerontius*. The Last Sacraments have been administered, the priest has said *Proficiscere*, and Gerontius has died in the state of grace. The guardian angel's final task is to bring his soul to the particular judgement, and so to purgatory, and thence to heaven. His song is Alleluia.

> My work is done,
> My task is o'er,
> And so I come,
> Taking it home,
> For the crown is won,
> Alleluia,
> For evermore.
>
> My Father gave
> In charge to me
> This child of earth
> E'en from its birth,
> To serve and save,
> Alleluia,
> And saved is he.

> This child of clay
> To me was given,
> To rear and train
> By sorrow and pain
> In the narrow way,
> Alleluia,
> From earth to Heaven.[7]

According to St Thomas, while we are still on the road to the heavenly Jerusalem, our guardian angel protects us from danger within and without, for, as it says in the Psalm, "in this way wherein I walked, they have hidden a snare for me" (141:4). If we have died in the state of grace and, if need be, undergone final cleansing in purgatory, then, says St Thomas, we have an angel to reign with us in heaven. If we have died in the state of unrepented mortal sin, rejecting the divine mercy, then we have a demon to punish us in hell.[8]

A HAPPY ENDING

By the mercy of our Creator and Redeemer, the drama of human history is a divine *comedy*. It has a happy ending. There will be a *penultimate* catastrophe: the collapse of the physical order, wars, plagues, and Antichrist's deceiving of many of the elect.[9] But finally, all shall be well, all manner of thing shall be well, for all manner of thing cooperates for the good for those who love God (cf. Rom 8:28). The incarnate Son will come again on the last day of human history with the angels of His power (cf. 2 Thess 1:7; Mt 16:27), the perpetual ministers of His almighty justice and infinite mercy. The Lord Jesus, risen gloriously from the dead, will slay Antichrist with the spirit of His mouth (cf. 2 Thess 2:8), destroy the last enemy, which is death (cf. 1 Cor 15:26), and throw into the lake of fire Satan and those who have died believing Satan's lies (cf. Apoc 19:20; 21:8). But from the eyes of the elect,

---

7   St John Henry Newman, "The Dream of Gerontius," in *Verses on Various Occasions*, 335.

8   Cf. *ST* 1a q. 113, a. 4.

9   See 107–10 above.

the little ones of God, He will wipe away every tear, "and death shall be no more" (Apoc 21:4). The pure of heart will be happy forever with the Blessed Trinity, the ever-virgin Mother of the eternal Son, and all the saints. They will share the beatitude of the angels in festal gathering in the City of the living God, "where security is assured, tranquility secure, where mirth is tranquil, eternity happy, happiness eternal, where there is perfect love and no fear, where eternal salvation abounds and truth reigns, where there is no deceiving or being deceived, where all things are good."[10] In this bliss, human souls, and after the resurrection complete human persons, will be the *equals* of the angels, as our Lord promises (cf. Lk 20:36), not by nature, but through God's generous gifts of grace and glory. "There will not be two societies of men and angels," says St Thomas, following St Augustine, "but one, because the blessedness of all is cleaving to the one God."[11]

To the eternal frustration of the proud spirits, and for the definitive refutation of the angelistic absurdities of the Manichees and Cartesians, Christ our Lord will at the end make men and women, as He is, radiantly immortal and indestructibly happy *in the body*. He will conform their lowly bodies to His glorious body (cf. Phil 3:21). The completion of the adoption of the sons of Adam as the sons of God will be "the redemption of the body" (cf. Rom 8:23). In their glorious freedom (cf. Rom 8:21), they will be free in the flesh from disease and disability but will retain in their final flourishing the God-given maleness and femaleness of their birth.[12] They will share heaven's glory with the angels, but as men and women of flesh and blood, not as bodiless spirits. God will fill the ruined ranks of the angelic choirs with just men made perfect, blessed in soul and in their bodies shining like the sun in the Kingdom of the Father (cf. Mt 13:43).

On the last day, the Son of God will come with His angels to signify the humility of His Incarnation and Passion, for by His death in the flesh He became a little less than the angels

---

10 St Boniface of Mainz, *Sermo* 13; PL 89.868A.
11 St Thomas, *ST* 1a q. 108, a. 8.
12 Cf. *Sent.* lib. 4, d. 44, q. 1, a. 3, qa. 4.

(cf. Ps 8:6); He comes as Son of Man. But He also comes with His angels in manifestation of His divinity. "They are his angels. He created them. He is the angels' Lord, not by comparison, as the Arians imagine, as if he were the greatest one of them, but Lord by the divinity and majesty in which he is coequal with the Father, and so he is said to come with *his* angels in the glory of the Father."[13] And, when He arrives again on earth, His angels will have a humble task to perform in the service of God and the redemption of the human body, as St Thomas explains. Three powers will be at work in the resurrection of the dead: "the divine power, and the power of Christ's humanity (for His Resurrection is the cause of our resurrection, as the Apostle says, 'as in Adam all die, so in Christ all will rise again' [1 Cor 15:22]). The angelic power will also be at work for certain preliminaries, namely, collecting the dust."[14]

After this gathering up of human frailty and its refashioning in glory, when the angels of Christ the King have separated the evil and unrepentant from the just and contrite (cf. Mt 13:49f), the Divine Comedy will reach its final scene, the Eighth Day that knows no sunset. Then the players of the great drama, Adam's sons and daughters redeemed by the Blood of the Lamb and gloriously embodied, and the ever-faithful holy angels, will live happily ever after with Mary Immaculate, the cause of their joy. They will see and love, love and praise, the Trinitarian God of Love, who moves the sun and the other stars. "And all the angels stood about the throne and the ancients and the four

---

13 St Paschasius Radbertus, *Expositio in evangelium Matthaei*, lib. 8; PL 120. 574B.

14 St Thomas, *Super Matthaeum* cap. 24, lect. 3. "Augustine says that, just as lower and thicker bodies are ruled in a certain order by more subtle and powerful bodies, so bodies are certainly ruled by God through the rational spirit of life. Gregory touches on this in *Dialogues* 4. Therefore, in all the bodily things done by God, God uses the ministry of the angels. Now in the resurrection something happens to transform bodies, namely, the collection of the ashes and their preparation for the restoration of the human body. For this task, then, in the resurrection God will employ the ministry of angels. But since the soul is created immediately by God, so it is united to the body immediately by God, without anything being done by the angels" (St Thomas, *Sent.* lib. 4, d. 43, q. 1, a. 2, qa. 3).

living creatures. And they fell down before the throne upon their faces and adored God, saying: 'Amen. Benediction and glory and wisdom and thanksgiving, honor and power and strength, to our God, forever and ever. Amen'" (Apoc 7:11–12).

INDEX·OF·NAMES

ABOUT·THE·AUTHOR

Fr. John Saward is priest-in-charge of the parish of SS. Gregory and Augustine, Oxford, which for many years was the parish of J. R. R. Tolkien. He is a former teacher of dogmatic theology at Catholic institutions in England, the United States, and Austria, and author of eight other books, including *The Beauty of Holiness and the Holiness of Beauty* and *Cradle of Redeeming Love* (both published by Angelico Press).

www.ingramcontent.com/pod-product-compliance
Lightning Source LLC
Chambersburg PA
CBHW032059080426

42733CB00006B/334